The Eccentric Cookbook

The Eccentric Cookbook

A Feast of Entertaining Recipes and Amusing Information About People and Food

RICHARD, EARL OF BRADFORD

ILLUSTRATED BY MERRILY HARPUR

Robson Books

Acknowledgements

Anthony Jackson's Boiled Sheep's Head, Isobel White's Australian Aboriginal Damper and The Whistling Steak, Stephen and Roxane Gudeman's Ropa Vieja and Lindsay Verrier's Coconut Leaf Cookery are reproduced from *The Anthropologists' Cookbook* (1977), edited by Jessica Kuper, by kind permission of Routledge and Kegan Paul.

Barry Humphries' Ednawiches are reproduced from *Writers' Favourite Recipes* (1978), The National Book League Anthology compiled by Gillian Vincent, by kind permission of Corgi Books.

Recipes from *The Roman Cookery Book* (1958) by Barbara Flower and Elisabeth Rosenbaum are reproduced by kind permission of Harrap Ltd.

Mock Champagne is reproduced from *The Victorian Cookery Book* (1975) edited by Gordon Grimley, published by Abelard-Schuman Ltd, by kind permission of Blackie & Son Ltd.

Designed by Harold King

First Published October 1985
Reprinted December 1985

First Published in the United Kingdom in 1985 by
Robson Books Ltd., Bolsover House, 5–6 Clipstone Street
London W1P 7EB.
Copyright © 1985 Richard, Earl of Bradford.

British Library Cataloguing in Publication Data

Bradford, Richard Thomas Orlando Bridgeman, *Earl of*
    The eccentric cookbook: a feast of entertaining recipes
    and amusing information about people and food.
    1. Cookery
    I. Title
    641.5   TX663

ISBN 0-86051-354-8

Printed and bound in Great Britain by Bell & Bain Ltd., Glasgow

Contents

Introduction

As you can no doubt tell from my figure I have an abiding interest in food. I started off at Cambridge preparing three-course dinner parties on two gas rings but it's funny what took me into the restaurant business eventually – I was fired by enthusiasm on my way back from Australia after spending four months in hospital with a broken back!

I came back through California, in 1971, and apart from being stopped at LA Airport as a suspected terrorist because of all the metal in my back (the customs officer said 'OK, buddy, where's the metal?' and I had to reply, 'You'll never find it!') I much admired the very pleasant family-style restaurants in California, unlike anything in Britain. I arrived back in London and found that they were being introduced there, with The Great American Disaster and Hard Rock Café, and so I opened an American-style restaurant in Brighton called Leadbelly – after the blues singer rather than the quality of the food! I believe it is still there today, next door to the Theatre Royal.

I also had Bewicks in Walton Street, which during that time gained an Egon Ronay Star. I shall never forget one incredible week – we had a brigade of four in the kitchen and on the Monday night the chef had a heart attack; on Thursday the third chef walked out complaining that the assistant chef was touching her up; and on the Saturday night with a completely full restaurant, at 9 pm, having been temporarily promoted, the second chef collapsed in a heap on the floor. We gave him two double brandies, put him on his feet and he worked the evening out. We did not open for normal business on Monday.

I owned the Caviar Bar in Knightsbridge for some years and at the moment, as well as owning Porters in Covent Garden, my culinary energies are mainly taken up in organizing and cooking gourmet dinners at Weston Park. This is a house which has been in our family for centuries but we have the usual problems of stately home owners and my wife and I actually live in a house just outside the estate and run Weston very much as a business. I am very fortunate in having already gained expertise in catering as it has undoubtedly helped me in putting the house on a good business footing.

However, although catering is a business, it does still remain very much a personal interest. Over the years, beginning when I was working in Ghana on VSO and later on my travels to other far-flung corners of the globe, I began to collect recipes and anecdotes about food. These were generally of a rather eccentric nature and I continued adding to my collection back in England, often finding English examples among old cookery books. An interest in eccentric recipes not unnaturally led to an interest in eccentric people and it is quite amazing how many eccentricities are connected with food (or with going round accompanied by

your coffin before death, but we'll gloss over that). Eccentric recipes, eccentric people and an interest in my own ancestors produced some rather satisfying discoveries, most interesting being Elizabeth Mytton, a relative of mad Squire Mytton's and an ancestress of mine, and Humphrey Kynaston, a curious Robin Hood figure whose cave hide-out is still on the estate. Eventually I thought it would be fun to put this strange collection into book form and, looking at what it contained – and perhaps also at me – a friend suggested calling it *The Eccentric Cookbook*. I think it is an entirely apt title for a cookbook like this one: eclectic, full of amusing information and fascinating facts about people and food, including some recipes you'll long to try out and many you'll be happier just to read. Because this is very much my own collection and the sort of cook book to read and dip into rather than to use as a Bible when Grannie comes for Sunday lunch, I have left all the recipes more or less in their original form, feeling it would be counter to the essence of the book to reduce such culinary delights as Lamb's Blood Pudding, Stamp and Go, Pooloot and Desperate Dan's Cow Pie to a standard formula which takes into account metric and imperial measurements.

My especial thanks to all those friends (I won't call them eccentric friends, but certainly interesting personalities) who sent in their own contributions when they heard about my project. If any readers have any outrageous recipes to add to my collection I shall be delighted to receive them. Meanwhile, to round off this introduction and to introduce the rest of the book in the right frame of mind, let me present a little ditty composed by talented composer/lyricist Grant Baynham who, like me, thinks that food is more enjoyable if it isn't taken too seriously.

Wipe That Round Yer Wok

Stage One

You take a slice of tripe
A brace of snipe
And a mango (slightly over-ripe)
Some pâté ardennes and a leek julienne
And a fenugreek with a little cayenne.
Slop the lot in a copper-bottomed pot,
With a shot of decent hock.
Salt to taste
Reduce to a paste
And wipe *that* round yer wok.

Stage Two

You take two quail's eggs
Two frog's legs
Pulverize a pullet's egg and purée the dregs.
Ask a fishmonger to liquefy the lung
Of a ling with a nice long conger-eel's tongue
Braise a bit of basil
'Till it's burnt to a frazzle,
And bash it on a butcher's block.
Mix all that
With a lump of fat
And wipe *that* round yer wok.

You're doing – Nouvelle Cuisine
You joined the club
It's not like cooking,
It's more like mucking around with decent, honest grub
Hooray for pretty-looking,
Witty cooking – art at its most fleeting –
If you're fond of food
But find it boring eating.

Then! Stage Three
You take some kiwi fruit
Some bamboo shoot
Simmer with a sliver of liverwort root
And dill, in a gill of gin-and-it
With a bit of goat's udder (that's the *real* tit-bit)
Some langoustines
And a single Heinz baked bean
In a good white stock
Add olive oil
Bring to the boil
And wipe *that* round yer wok

Then! Shakespearean Stage the Fourth
You take fillet of the fenny snake
In the cauldron boil and bake
Adder's fork and blind worm's sting
Lizard's leg and howlet's wing
Wool of bat and eye of newt, fresh wrenched from its socket
I'd have mentioned scale of dragon
But your grocer may not stock it . . . .

You're doing – Nouvelle Cuisine
It's all prepared!
The ingredients are ready!
I can hear you smack your lips!
Now!
Beat the eggs and meat and fish
Briskly into doggy's dish, . . .
And cook yourself a plate of egg and chips.

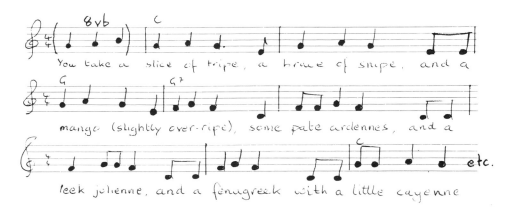

An Eccentric Menu From Bruce Green
Renowned Party Giver, Prankster
And Elephant Polo Aficionado

Order of Serving
Volcanic Strawberry Pudding
Peacock Panache *and* Lotus Root Salad
Fish: 'Fangs For the Memory'
Elephant Consommé

Beverages
Fire Eater *or* Thawed Himalayan Mountain Ice

VOLCANIC STRAWBERRY PUDDING

300 g (12 oz) strawberries
250 ml (½ a pint) whipping cream
100 g (4 oz) caster sugar
One tablespoon strawberry dacquiri

Extra whole strawberries
Squeeze of lemon juice
Small piece (250 g) of dry ice
(solid carbon dioxide).

Crush strawberries, sprinkle with caster sugar, add squeeze of lemon juice, Leave for one hour. Whip cream until stiff, fold in fruit and the juice. Pour mixture into straight-sided soufflé dish and place in deep freezer or freezing compartment. When partially frozen, remove and beat thoroughly – this prevents water crystals forming. Return to fridge in a strawberry mould if possible.

Remove from fridge. Scoop out base to leave a hollow large enough for the 'dry ice'. With care and gloves break up the dry ice and arrange in a small heap in centre of a silver tray. Remove pudding from mould by inverting mould over dry ice mound on the tray. Arrange whole fruit around pudding and on top – crush if desired. Place silver tray on a lighted food warmer. With a straw pierce several holes in pudding to allow dry ice smoke to escape – visually very exciting. Also tastes good.

Warning: do not allow the dry ice to touch your skin – and do not serve any.

PEACOCK PANACHE

One large Malaysian blue peacock
(male by definition). Do not hang.
One measure of patna rice
Half measure of grated coconut
One whole lime

Half measure of peanuts (not salted)
Four chopped livers (peacock or
chicken)
Rose water

Carefully remove peacock head and neck complete, avoiding loss of feathers, put on one side. Remove wings carefully preserving feathers. With care pluck tail feathers and hold for serving. Defeather body and remove entrails – wash out. Chop and blend stuffing ingredients above with a small amount of rose water (1 tablespoon). Fill carcass generously with stuffing – paint outside of peacock with coconut oil – sparingly. Place some *small* coriander leaves on the rib cage. Place in baking tray with cloves in bottom of tray. Cover with foil – cook in medium heat oven for approx. 15 minutes per pound. Do not remove foil or brown.

Using silver platter covered with vine leaves place the cooked peacock centrally. With a skewer fix the head erect. Place wings in natural position. Using small Ogen melon insert the decorative tail feathers in a display/fan arrangement. Serve with much gusto in a vaulted room.

LOTUS ROOT SALAD

1 lotus root
1 tablespoon vinegar
½ cup sake
4 tablespoons sugar

¾ cup of water
½ teaspoon salt
2 red peppers

Clean and peel lotus root and cut it into slices about ¼ in thick. Put immediately into cold water with a little vinegar. Stops discoloration. Put lotus root with water in small saucepan and bring to boil. Cook for two/three minutes until the skins are tender but still crisp. Remove from fire and drain. Put the sake, sugar water and salt into a saucepan and bring to boil. When sugar has dissolved remove from fire and pour over lotus root slices. Allow to stand for 20 minutes. Drain and chill. Can be served with very thin slices of red pepper for added visual effect.

FANGS FOR THE MEMORY

Head and 6–9 ins of large python
(best fresh, second best frozen)
3 sea bream
3 large prawns
12 fresh mushrooms

6 chestnuts
Salt
Lemon
Pine needles

Carefully remove the flesh by making an incision along the stomach and peeling back the skin. Scrape flesh out, being careful not to damage the skin – remove bone structure. Wash out and discard flesh. Blend delicately the bream, prawns, mushrooms and chestnuts. Lay the mixture on a bed of fresh pine needles and salt liberally. Cover the dish with aluminium foil. Bake in hot oven 400° F for 20 mins.

After baking arrange in a heaped strip on a fresh bed of pine needles. The snake head and skin are draped over the baked fish. Serving is via the snake's mouth. This should be fixed open with wooden cocktail sticks on each side of the jaw. The flavour is beautiful, with the aroma of pine and the visual delights of pink and dark green making it a fitting dish for the most formal occasion. The snake head adds visual confusion to the flavour.

ELEPHANT CONSOMMÉ

300 gms/12 oz shin of elephant
(Indian, African too gamey)
1 litre/2 pints good stock
Seasoning
1 celery top

2 in piece of cinnamon stick
3 bay leaves
Dash of paprika
Peach brandy

Cut the meat into small sections and put into saucepan with stock and other ingredients. Gently simmer for one hour. Strain through several thicknesses of silk stockings. Add one dessertspoon of peach brandy to each dish – and drink.

FIRE EATER

1 teacup fresh coconut milk
1 teacup sake (Nada or Hiroshima)
1 egg white

1 tablespoon honey
Pinch of salt
2 fresh lychees

Mix above vigorously in liquidizer to form viscous white base. Pour into fine cut glass bowl to about ¼ full. Add slowly a litre of fine crushed ice. Finally top with care the ice with best Russian vodka (high octane). The vodka is set alight and the concoction drunk slowly through a glass or wax – *not* plastic – straw.

SOUPS
SNACKS
AND STARTERS

Wings on the Doorstep

In 1965–66 when I was seventeen I taught on VSO as a junior maths master in Ghana. Thanks to the revolution when Nkrumah was kicked out I achieved a quick promotion to senior (and only) chemistry master, teaching A-level and ended up doing just about everything: I compiled the staff weekly circular, ran the football club, was house junior master, ran the school dancing club; but I don't remember what I did in my spare time!

I lived in the dormitory block and when it rained the ants came in their thousands. They can fly for only six hours, then they lose their wings and mate furiously. From the compounds around the natives would suddenly appear with buckets of water, grab handfuls of preoccupied ants, drown them and then cook them over their fires, leaving masses of discarded wings all over your doorstep.

They tell me fried ants are crunchy and nutty tasting, although I never ate them. I lost three stone in three months, partly due to being in hospital with typhus fever and malaria. There's really only myself to blame for that. Among my responsibilities I was dispensary master. At one point we ran out of proprietary malaria pills so I had to give them my own supply – and promptly went down with the disease! I've a terrible feeling I wasn't the only one.

FRIED WHITE ANTS

4 oz 1–2 day-old white ants	$\frac{1}{4}$ pint water
2 tsps groundnut oil or butter	Salt to taste

Clean the ants by removing wings and any grit. Put ants in a pan and add the salt and water. Boil rapidly for about ten minutes or until the water evaporates. Reduce the heat, add the oil or butter. Cover the saucepan to let the oil be absorbed. Remove from the heat – serve hot.

Serves two.

The following is a variation on the same theme but is an East African recipe.

FRIED GRASSHOPPERS OR LOCUSTS

1 lb 1–2 day-old locusts or grasshoppers
8 oz groundnut oil or butter

1 pint of water
Salt to taste

Remove the limbs and wings from the insects. Put the locusts/grasshoppers in a heavy pan with the salt and water. Simmer for about 30 minutes, or until the insects are soft. Boil rapidly until the water has evaporated. Lower the heat, and add half the oil or butter. Cook over a low heat until the insects are crisp. Add the remaining oil and cook five minutes more. Remove from the heat, serve hot with ugali or matoke.

Serves four.

John Bratby

Royal Academician John Bratby is truly an eccentric artist as they are always imagined to be. He lives in a house where every room is crammed with his paintings, many of them the beautiful sunflowers which he has made almost a trademark of his. John Bratby is not just a painter, he is also a thinker. Some years ago he came to the conclusion that originality was doomed to extinction as the technological age advances and he started a collection of paintings of people whom he considered truly individual. I am gratified that he has included me in their number. Anyone who goes to sit for Bratby is entertained at lunch with one of his delightful wife Patti's bacon sandwiches, which she calls Bratby's Bacon Butties. Nothing could be more delicious after a hard morning sitting down.

BRATBY'S BACON BUTTIES

Scrape 2 slices of matching sized bread right up
to and over the crusts with Flora.
Put under grill with 2 generous slices back bacon.
WATCH.
Should all be done about the same time. Nicely
browned.
Scrape the untoasted sides of the bread with butter
or marg right up to the edge. Be generous with the
bacon.
Sometimes put in tomato & lettuce, making a BLT.
Serve on Dresden China plate. Decorate with dainty
blue borage flower or similar from herb garden.
Give enough coloured paper serviettes to guest.

Terry Wogan

Terry Wogan, broadcaster extraordinaire, is the Irishman with the gift of the gab who seems virtually to have taken over the airwaves in this country – and no bad thing in my opinion. This recipe is remarkably simple.

MURPHY'S REVENGE

Take two slices of fresh crusty white bread. Spread liberally
with butter. Fill with sizzling hot freshly fried chips – season.
Add dressing to taste. EAT!

John Bratby, RA., ARCA., RBA., FIAL., FRSA.

BRATBY'S BACON BUTTIES

This is what I do:

Scrape 2 slices of matching sized bread right up to + over the crusts with Flora.

Put under grill with 2 generous slices back bacon. WATCH.

Should all be done about the same time. Nicely browned.

Scrape the untoasted sides of the bread with butter or marg right up to the edge. Be generous with the bacon. Sometimes put in tomato + lettuce, making a BLT.

Serve on Dresden china plate. Decorate with dainty blue borage flower or similar from herb garden. Give enough coloured paper serviettes to guest.

Love
Patti xx

Wally Herbert

On his rare visits to civilization Wally Herbert (more on him in the *Meat Dishes* section) is particularly fond of Crofters' Eggs, a dish devised by Brian Stamp, formerly executive chef at the now defunct Hilton International at Stratford-on-Avon.

CROFTERS' EGGS

2 poached eggs
4 oz lobster sauce

$2\frac{1}{2}$ oz flaked cooked Scotch
salmon
$\frac{1}{2}$ oz grated Cheddar cheese

Place flaked salmon on the bottom of the egg dish, and pour the hot lobster sauce over it. Allow to simmer until salmon is hot. Place two poached eggs on the top of the salmon, lightly dress with grated cheese, then flash quickly under the salamander to glaze. Garnish with fresh parsley and serve at once.

Frederick William Densham

Parsimonious Mr Densham, vicar of Warleggan in Cornwall, never visited his parishioners. He kept them at bay with a tall fence and fierce dogs; they ceased churchgoing. He propped cardboard cutouts of them in the pews and is said to have preached his final sermon before these and five others, including two reporters. He died in 1953 – perhaps from his diet of nettles and porridge?

NETTLES

Nettles can be eaten as a vegetable, like spinach, and need not be dressed up into a fancy recipe. Perhaps wearing rubber gloves, wash the nettles several times in cold water. Put into a saucepan with a very little water and boil them until tender. Rub them through a sieve, add a knob of butter and sprinkle over some salt and black pepper.

By the way, only the young tender shoots are suitable for eating in this way.

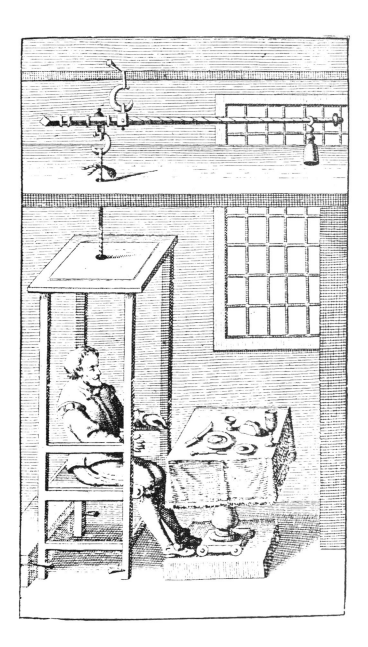

Near and Far

Two recipes, one collected during my memorable time in Africa, the other an old Scots dish made on much the same lines, proving that things aren't so different whether you live on the Equator or in the frozen North. I have not persuaded my wife that we should try out either of them!

COW BLOOD COOKED IN FRESH MILK

3 pints cow's blood
4 oz ghee or margarine
Salt to taste

$\frac{1}{2}$ pint fresh milk
1 small chopped onion, optional

Stir and separate the liquid blood from the clot. Fry the onion in a heavy pan in half the ghee or margarine until brown. Mix the blood with the milk and add to the pan with the onion. Cook over a low heat, stirring to prevent burning. Add more milk if the mixture becomes too thick. Add the remaining ghee and the salt. Cover the saucepan, lower the heat and simmer for about 15 minutes. Remove from the heat and serve hot with bread or boiled rice.

Serves two–three.

LAMB'S BLOOD PUDDING

Blood, cream, salt, spice, mint, chives or young onions, fat.

Take as much blood as with half a mutchkin (half a pint) of cream will fill an ashet; mix the blood and cream together and run through a search. Season with salt and spices, a sprig of mint and chives or young onions, minced small; mince the fat of the near or kidney small; mix all together and fire in the oven or in a frying-pan

Lamb's blood is the sweetest of all blood.

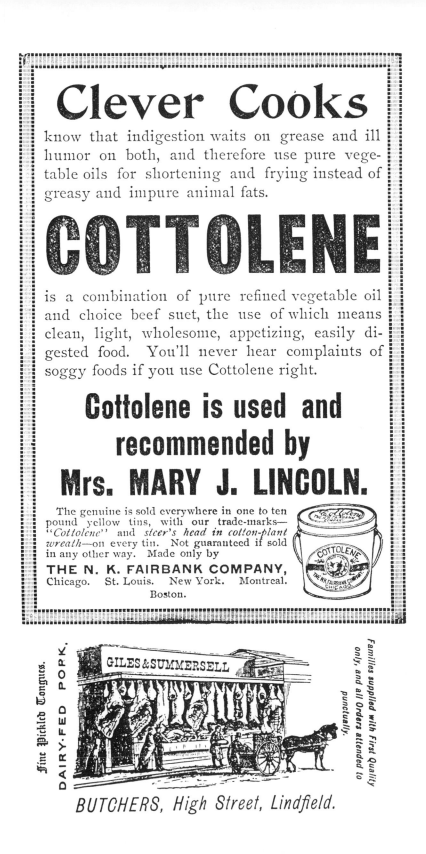

Damper is an even more authentic Australian recipe than kangaroo, and is eaten by the Aborigines. This is a recipe as written down by anthropologist Isobel White.

AUSTRALIAN ABORIGINAL DAMPER

1   Retrieve your axe from whomever has borrowed it, collect plenty of firewood and make up the camp-fire, so that it is 3 or 4 four feet in diameter and burning brightly. I suspect there are few firewoods in the world so hot and clear burning as some of the Australian acacias. Where I lived with Aborigines the firewood used was Western Myall (*Acacia sowdenii*). (This wood is used to make native artefacts, the main source of income for these Aborigines; they are famous for their careful craftsmanship, and their products are sold all over the world; this activity leaves much waste wood, which is used for fires when dry and seasoned.)

2   Find a large pan or dish. This may be the hardest task of all. In a society unused to such items there never seems any place to keep them in the native bough shelters. In any case no woman can refuse to lend hers to a neighbour or refuse to hand it to any young child who wants it to make play dampers of earth and water. Having found a pan and shaken off the sand or dirt put there by the child, put in some flour, some salt and some baking powder ('some' means about 5 lb (2.5 kilos) flour, a couple of tbsp baking powder (about 2 oz./60 grams) and the same of salt.

3   Go and get some water (if you can find a bucket – the same process may be necessary as for the pan). The one water-tank kept filled by the mission water-truck is probably two or three hundred yards away, so it might have been better to get it first of all. N.B. While away getting water, make quite sure that the pan of flour is out of reach of children and dogs, or you will have to start the whole process again (if you still have any flour left). It would be much better if you could persuade a younger woman or a girl to fetch the water. Don't ask a man or a boy, as it is demeaning for a male to carry water.

4   Now add enough water to the flour to make a stiff dough. Spread an old flour-sack on the ground, turn the dough on to it and knead well.

5   Shape into a cake about 2 inches thick and perfectly round, about the size of a large bicycle wheel. (My teacher could make them so symmetrical that they looked machine made.) N.B. Fend off dogs and children all the time. The children will want to pinch off pieces of dough. One dog will take the lot. This anthropologist once lost the whole of her supper while her back was turned for seconds.

6   Pull the fire aside. It should by now have burned down to hot coals. Rake flat an area of hot ash and place the damper on it. Cover with more hot ash (about 1 inch thick) and leave for 20 or 30 minutes. Jets of steam can be seen breaking through the hot ash during the cooking, and when there is no more steam, the damper is done. Remove from ashes and brush off adhering charcoal, ash and sand. This damper is delicious eaten hot with butter and jam, syrup or honey. Some of my Aboriginal friends dunk it in very sweet tea.

Orde Wingate

It isn't often that the British Army tolerates someone as maverick as Orde Wingate, but he was a highly valued and successful officer. This paradox extended to his love of the New Testament – he once ordered a consignment of rams' horns to frighten the Arab enemy (à la Gideon). He fully expected the mission to fail when bugles were delivered instead – and it did!

His insistence on conducting Army business without any clothes on was enough to put any but the most unmindful visitor off. He spurned bathing, rank and uniform. When he occasionally *had* to wear uniform, it would be so dirty as to express perfectly his contempt for the required formality.

Wingate spent much of his Army career in the Middle East, and believed that raw onions, occasionally supplemented by grapes, were the key to retaining one's health in the heat. If you think the flavour of this onion salad might be too strong, try adding seedless grapes.

ONION SALAD

4 large onions
4 tbs salt
1 tsp vinegar
1½ tbs lemon juice

1½ tsp water
3 tbs olive oil
1 tbs chopped parsley
salt and pepper

Peel onions and slice very thinly lengthwise. Put the slices in a sieve or colander (overlapping as little as possible) and sprinkle on the salt. Press onions and salt together with a wooden spoon or spatula until the salt is dissolved. Rinse the onions in cold running water. Leave to drain well. Mix the vinegar, lemon juice and water in a wooden salad bowl. Season to taste. Gradually whisk in the olive oil until the dressing is thick and creamy. Add the onions and parsley and mix thoroughly. Mix again just before serving.

Serves four.

Early Starters

The Roman cookery writer Apicius (more on him in the *Poultry and Game* section) covered a wide range of methods and ingredients. Two thousand years later snails are still a popular starter, although more so on the continent than in Britain. The Romans introduced edible snails to this country and used to breed them on their camp-sites – just left them to roam loose. Within a few hundred yards of a former Roman camp you can still find edible snails. On a sunny afternoon after a summer rain go out with your bucket and collect them.

I'm terribly sorry if you catch the wrong ones – edible snails are fatter and more juicy.

COCLEAS – SNAILS

COCLEAS LACTE PASTAS: accipies cocleas, spongizabis, membranam tolles, ut possint prodire. adicies in vas lac et salem uno die, ceteris diebus [in] lac per se, et omni hora mundabis stercus. cum pastae fuerint, ut non possint se retrahere, ex oleo friges. mittes oenogarum.

SNAILS FED ON MILK. Take the snails, clean with a sponge, remove the membrane so that they may come out [of their shells]. Put in a vessel [with the snails] milk and salt for one day, for the following days add only milk, and clean away the excrements every hour. When the snails are fattened to the point that they cannot get back [into their shells] fry them in oil. Serve with *oenogarum**.

*A seasoning of pepper, lovage, coriander, rue, *liquamen*, honey, wine, and a little oil, or: thyme, savory, pepper, lovage, honey, wine, *liquamen*, and oil. *Liquamen* seems to have been a pungent liquid made by reducing a strong fishy brine, seasoned with oregano, and sometimes containing wine: it was made in quantity, stored and used as needed.

Not Recommended

I have to include Lord Woolton in this book for the pie he introduced to British cooks when he was Minister of Food during the Second World War. His brief in 1943 was to provide food, housing and work. A series of recipe books was produced, with recipes making the most of what was available throughout the country. 'Woolton Pie' was one of these and although I give the Ingredients and Mode (to follow Mrs Beeton) it is not a recipe I urge you to try!

WOOLTON PIE

Ingredients: carrots, parsnips, potatoes and turnips. Mode: Place these in a pastry case. Top the pie with a thick white sauce and bake until cooked.

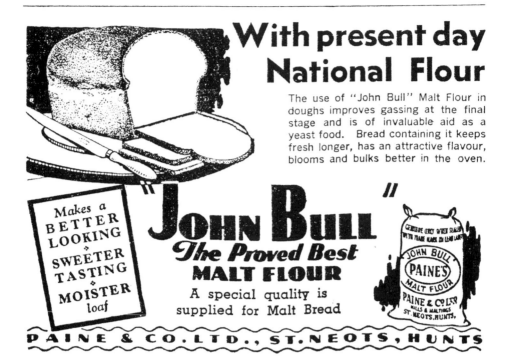

Dame Edna Everage

Dame Edna leaves most of us at a loss for words. Superstar, but ordinary housewife too, she treads the tightrope between invitations to No. 10 and looking after her husband Norm as only the most famous lady Australian could do. Although it may not be *comme il faut* to mention a lady's age, I was genuinely amazed that the wonderful Dame Edna is fifty. Who would believe it when you see her so exquisitely gowned and bespectacled?

I am so pleased that, in consultation with Barry Humphries, she allowed me to reproduce her famous Ednawiches recipe – these will turn any picnic into a real experience!

EDNAWICHES

Sandwich fillings need not be dull, for Australia has pioneered some delicious and exotic sambie*-centres. When making sambies remember that in most cases they have to travel a long way in hot little boxes before they get gobbled up for lunch. There's nothing worse, is there readers, than a horrid dry crumbly sambie? So, remember my Golden Rule and use the moistest possible ingredients. Here is a particularly tasty filling as a lunch-hour thrill for kiddies and senior citizens alike: 1 sweet eating apple, 2 snowballs (to be bought at any lolly shop), slices of bread. Peel and core the sweet apple. Cut into thin slices, *taking care that there is no taint of onion on your chopping board.* Spread on to thin slices of buttered white bread. Cut snowballs into thin slices and spread above apple, cover with another slice of buttered bread, and stick sandwich firmly together by hand, *taking care that there is no taint of onion on the palm.* (Garlic is also a non-desirable odour to invade this dish. Not even New Australians would think that nice.)

*Sambies – an increasingly popular diminutive for sandwiches. Variant: sambos, less frequently used.

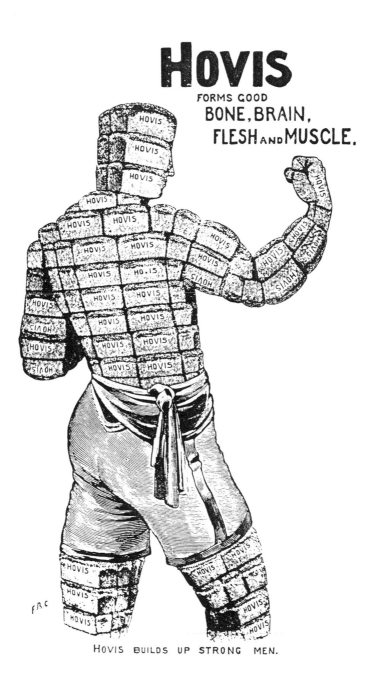

HOVIS

FORMS GOOD
BONE, BRAIN,
FLESH AND MUSCLE.

HOVIS BUILDS UP STRONG MEN.

COOKERY.

NECESSITY FOR LEARNING.

As an education, cookery is happily becoming more common every day, and not only are we shown in the schools for the purpose how to bake, boil or stew various foods, but the *reasons why* for doing these things, how to combine the right kinds of food and how to prepare everything in the best and most economical manner.

Excellence in the art is of course attained only by practice, experience and skill; but we hold it the duty of all women of middle class to know practically how to cook plain ordinary dishes, whether or no they ever attempt anything more ambitious in the way of cookery.

It is a knowledge that gives power whether we have to use it or not, and it is scarcely possible in theory to direct those under our authority to make dishes exactly as we require them if we can never show them by ocular demonstration what may be amiss.

Seldom too does it happen that necessity does not arise, some time or other, for the mistress or the daughters of a household to either give assistance or have to do some cooking alone; and for these emergencies it is well to be prepared.

Another argument in favour of knowing how to cook is that we can check waste or extravagance in those who cook for us, which we could not do if we were not sure from personal experience that, for example, three eggs would serve for one kind of dish where four were used, or that less butter was needed than had been employed in the making of another. In such little matters even the best of servants are apt to be indifferent till, service over, they come to cook for themselves.

EVERY-DAY MEALS.

TIMES FOR MEALS.

According to the occupations and ages of those for whom meals are prepared so must the hours for them be arranged; but there are two golden rules concerning them: namely, that there should be sufficient time allowed for them to be partaken of without hurry, and that they should be punctually served. Of little use is it having a dainty breakfast ready for the master of the house ten minutes before he has to start for business, or a well-cooked good dinner for the children when they have to hurry through it to be in time for afternoon school. Better is it to allow a little extra time than to run the risk of people having to bolt their food or go without it. There should always be a clear half-hour allowed for breakfast, and this should not be a meal that, as in many houses, runs on from eight to ten o'clock. This is fatal to the regular household routine; nor can breakfast be served comfortably and properly for different members keeping different times, unless it be in large households where there are many hands for the morning work.

The servants should be allowed time for their breakfast before that in the dining-room commences; and for them to do this it is absolutely necessary that they rise betimes. Children also should have an early breakfast, or there will be too long an interval between that and their tea of the day before. For master and mistress we cannot suggest a time, unless that it be not *later* than nine o'clock.

Where there are little ones and several servants, a dinner must be served in the middle of the day; but it is generally necessary to have some cooking done later when the master of the house returns. Most men who value their health prefer to have only a light luncheon during working hours and return to dinner late, and this is certainly more economical than dining away from home.

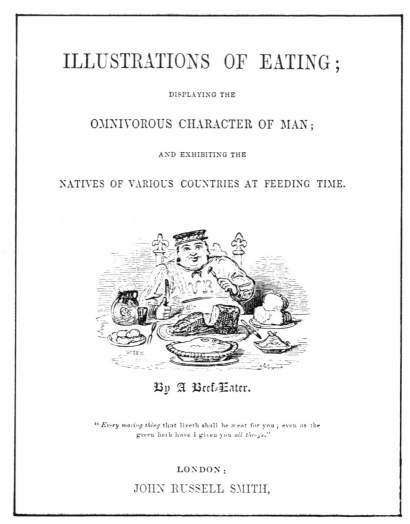

Hippopotamuses Don't Grow On Trees

My own eccentric ancestors seem positively normal
when compared to the father and son team of William
and Francis Trevelyan Buckland. Buckland *père* called
himself an 'undergroundologist', which meant he understood
more about geology, drain pipes, fossilized faeces and animal
droppings generally, than anyone. He put all this knowledge to
good use, of course, and had an extraordinary ability to identify
almost anything by smell. On one occasion, when he and a
friend were lost, he identified Uxbridge earth and so found their
way home.

But his most infamous deed concerned his good friend Edward Harcourt, Archbishop of York from 1808 to 1848. Harcourt had purchased Louis XIV's embalmed heart when he was in Paris during the Revolution, and showed it to Buckland. Whereupon Buckland took it out of the snuff-box in which Harcourt kept this treasure and swallowed it, saying 'I have eaten many things, but never the heart of a king.'

This penchant for eating very strange food must have been inherited. Buckland junior was a founder member of the Society for the Acclimatisation of Animals – a bold venture in the 1860s to persuade the British to be more experimental in their eating habits and ease shortages of conventional food. The menu for the Society's inaugural dinner included a soup made from Bird's Nest – Lawrence Leung of Zen restaurant in London has very generously given me a magnificent recipe for cooking this. There was also curried kangaroo.

Frank Buckland had an epicurean and scientific fascination with all animals, and would eat most of them except, surprisingly, horse. This creature he considered suitable only for stuffing and mounting in a showcase. His interest in animals was matched by his care and attention of human oddities, and his house was constantly filled with a variety of circus performers and mongooses, giants, dwarfs and wild animals. Buckland seems to have considered all alike as his friends and

but which knife & fork does one use?

pets, looking after them and furthering his curiousity about natural history. There is a wonderful story of a relative tripping over a dead baby hippopotamus in the dark, to be told by Buckland as he attended to both: 'You should be more careful. You might have damaged it. Hippopotamuses don't grow on trees, you know.'

DOUBLE-COLOURED STEWED BIRD'S NEST

80 g bird's nest

(a)	(b)
4 pieces ham	cornstarch
4 (large) black mushrooms	adequate amounts of lard
60 g bamboo shoot	and of minced chicken
1 carrot (boiled)	green peas
	320 g wax gourd
	8 (small) stalks spinach

1   Soak the bird's nest to raise and pluck fine hair away. Cut the (a) ingredients into shreds 2 mm wide and 6 cm long.
2   Apply a dash of lard to clean spoons and place a layer of minced chicken 5 mm thick on them; then lay two shreds each of the (a) ingredients in each spoon, with one end of each shred on the minced chicken (the other forms the bird's tail). Sprinkle on cornstarch, put the loose bird's nest on it, use green peas as the eyes half-buried in the bird's nest and steam the bird's nest in the steamer for 3 minutes.
3   Cut skinned wax gourd into rectangular pieces of 3 cm wide, 7 cm long and 1 mm thick, carve 3 mm square patterns on them with 8 mm left uncarved at each end, apply cornstarch on to them one by one, wrap them in cloth and steam them in the steamer for 5 minutes; transfer them into hot stock, boil them until done, take them out and pour cold boiled water over them.
4   Slide the bird's nests on to a serving plate, lay them on the rim with the head of one following the tail of the other, lay the boiled spinach covered with minced chicken side by side with the bird's nests and put the seasoned wax gourds in hot stock; season; stir in cornstarch solution and pour the sauce over the food.

MEAT DISHES

Colonel John Blashford-Snell, MBE

John Blashford-Snell is one of the world's most seasoned explorers and has been awarded medals in recognition of his leadership and direction of many expeditions. He launched Operation Drake with friends in 1978 – a huge, two-year adventure aimed at providing young people with a real challenge. Then, as in his new venture Operation Raleigh, the Colonel has received the support of the Prince of Wales.

When not working for the Ministry of Defence, John Blashford-Snell has a wide variety of interests which include writing, fishing, diving and jogging with his labrador. He loves Scotch whisky, wine, roast beef, and the films of Peter Sellers. According to his wife Judith, 'he snores like a pig and is impossible to sleep with!'

Whether you choose the Coward's Method or Blasher's Method of catching your crocodile for the recipe he offered me, it is not for the faint-hearted because you do, of course, have to be on one of his expeditions to cook it. John assures me *has* eaten 'croc' once – when rations ran out on the Blue Nile and they were all starving.

CROCODILE TEAS

'I was once at Paga in Africa, where there was a sacred crocodile pool. The guardians of the crocodiles who were living there, all ragged people, sold baby chickens to the tourists to lure the crocodiles, only the truth was they weren't lured by the chickens, but by the guardians whistling. We eventually cottoned on to this and so whistled next time we went.

'All the crocodiles came waddling out and the guardians were so furious that the gaffe had been blown we were banned from then on.'

BLUE NILE CROCODILE

(Only to be used in areas of crocodile over-population and with permission from the World Wildlife Fund)

Ingredients

**10 inches of prime crocodile tail (loose end)
casava plant
$\frac{1}{2}$ pint of cooking oil**

Method

Having chosen your crocodile (disguised in distance as floating log – but beware of real floating logs as these are not recommended for easy digestion) – you may then kill your prey.

Coward's method

Paddle up behind the beast as he lies asleep and gently, so as not to wake him, drop a hand grenade on his back. Be sure to catch the now detached tail, we don't want any foreign bodies from the bank of the Nile tarnishing the delicate flavour.

Blasher's method

Whoop for joy at spotting your dinner, and wave arms vigorously to attract his interest. He should cruise up to within an arm's length with an enquiring look to his mouth. As he grins up at you, swiftly insert the blade of your Swiss Army penknife into the back of his throat, drawing from left to right – ensuring that the incision is neat and clean (your taxidermist will be most grateful, and the finished article will look outstanding peering from your inglenook where lie many other relics from expeditioning).

Cooking instructions

Skin and fillet the meat into $2 \times \frac{1}{2}$ inch strips. Wrap each portion in casava (which should be in pulp form by now) and plunge into the sizzling oil. Cook for approximately 8 minutes, until golden brown all over.

NB:

For the perfectionist; try the added option of sprinkling leaf cutter ant's legs liberally on the pulp, and cook as above. This will add an interesting texture of a slightly crispy nature.

Richard Booth

Having started out as a mere bookseller in 1961, he is now the King of Hay-on-Wye! That's progress! His bookshop grew until it virtually swamped the small town of Hay-on-Wye in Herefordshire, on the Welsh borders, and Richard decided to begin a Home Rule movement for the town. People like Richard are true eccentrics, driven by some compulsion, and the publicity they get is only a side effect. Along the way Richard has been able to help a few friends of his up the social ladder, including April Ashley, who now flourishes as the Duchess of Hay. His ideas on food are as adamant as his ideas on everything else:

> I, myself, am only marginally keen on social eating, as I regard drinking, talking, riding a horse, and many other occupations as more worthy of passing the time. Eating I regard as one of the less important time consuming activities . . . equivalent perhaps to reading . . .
>
> My own belief on food is that it should be regional. Food sold on the Welsh border should be Welsh border food. If we eat Indian, Chinese, French, Italian, or, my especial dislike, the appalling so-called health food . . . we are inevitably inferior. I would, therefore, like to say that my especial favourites are home-cured bacon, faggots and peas, and cider made by myself. In even more detail I should like to specify that it should be cooked by the famous Mrs Ivy Lewis, who like myself is a Brecknock Borough Councillor. Needless to say, food prepared by one good working person is better than the food prepared by twenty university graduates (chemists, marketing, freezing, accountancy, promotions, etc.) at a supermarket. God save us from frozen meals.

CAWL, OR WELSH LAMB STEW

Take $1\frac{1}{2}$ lb middle neck of lamb, boil with 3 pints of water for about $\frac{3}{4}$ hour – leave until cold. At this stage it is possible to skim the fat from the top. Now add carrots, bring to the boil and cook for $\frac{1}{2}$ hour, then add 2 or 3 leeks, 1 lb onion, $1\frac{1}{2}$ lb potatoes, cut up small, and simmer for another hour. Add chopped parsley and/or dumplings, and serve.

When I wrote to him about the book, Richard also suggested an alcoholic's recipe from a friend and colleague, Frank English:

You soak a sheet in gin and chew it slowly through the night. You need an understanding wife for that one. Unfortunately, or maybe fortunately, I was not able to get in touch with one of his customers who was compiling a bibliography on British cannibalism, which included a recipe for British Officer Soup.

Next follows a recipe with a most strange-sounding name from Barbados. As with most things from that sunny island, it is wonderful!

JUG JUG

1 pt (2 glasses) pigeon peas
10 tbsp/good $\frac{1}{2}$ cup guinea
cornflour
4 oz fresh or salt beef
salt and pepper

4 oz lean pork
1 small onion
2/3 blades chives
thyme and parsley

Clean, cut up and season the beef and pork. If salt beef is used
it should be soaked. Stew the pork for 20 minutes, then add
beef and peas and stew for another half-hour or until peas are
soft. Strain off, but reserve the water, and mince or chop meat
and peas. Take $\frac{1}{2}$ pint (1 glass) of the water in which meat was
stewed, add meat and peas, and stir in the cornflour. Cook for
15–30 minutes, stirring all the time. The mixture should be
thick and smooth. Shape in a buttered basin and serve hot.

CHAPTER X.

Beef.

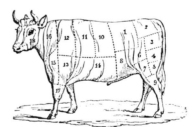

No.		No.	
1.	Sirloin.	11.	Middle Rib. (Four Ribs.)
2.	Rump.	12.	Chuck Rib. (Three Ribs.)
3.	Edge-bone.	13.	Shoulder, or Leg of Mutton
4.	Buttock, or Round.		Piece.
5.	Mouse Buttock.	14.	Brisket.
6.	Veiny Piece.	15.	Clod.
7.	Thick Flank.	16.	Neck.
8.	Thin Flank.	17.	Shin.
9.	Leg.	18.	Cheek.
10.	Fore Rib. (Five Ribs.)		

TO CHOOSE BEEF.

Beef is in reality in season through the entire year, but it is best during the
winter months, when it will hang a sufficient time to become tender before it is
dressed. Meat of a more delicate nature is better adapted for the table in summer. The *Christmas beef* of England is too much celebrated to require any
mention here.

LE GARDE-MANGER

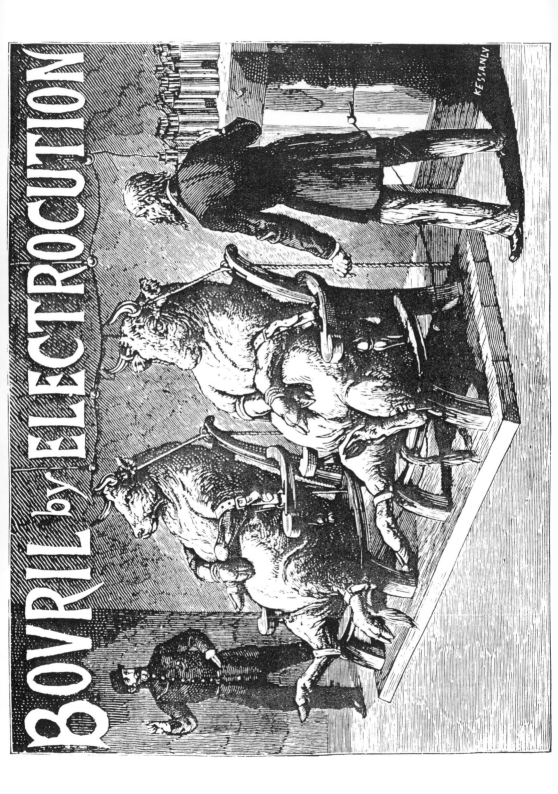

BOVRIL by ELECTROCUTION

Cyril Smith

One of the saving graces of British politics is that just when you think it's getting too serious it throws up an eccentric or two to relieve the gloom. Undoubtedly one of the larger-than-life characters in the House of Commons is Cyril Smith, who freely admits he loves his food. Born a Lancashire man, he naturally gave me a Lancashire recipe for my collection.

HOT POT

1 lb beef chuck steak cut into 1-inch pieces
1 gill water
6 medium potatoes peeled and sliced
4 medium onions peeled and sliced
6 carrots peeled and sliced
3 teaspoons salt
1×1 lb can tomatoes
$\frac{1}{2}$ teaspoon tabasco

Sprinkle beef with salt, brown thoroughly in a small amount of fat. Remove beef. Add water to fat in pan. Cook, stirring constantly to blend bits of meat left in pan. Remove from heat. Layer beef, potatoes, onions and carrots in casserole, sprinkling each layer with salt and a little tabasco, and adding tomatoes on each layer. Pour water and fat over (top layer being potato). Cook in medium oven (350–360° F) for at least 2 hours.

Serves six–eight

Note: This should be eaten with a pint of witches' brew to grease the throat.

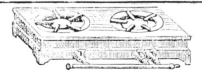

I added the following recipe to my collection from an original copy of Mrs Beeton. It was really the name that made it eligible – and I'm still not quite sure how you pronounce it! In the nineteenth century, Indian food was very fashionable in Britain and Mrs Beeton, who seemed to know everything there was to be known on the subject of cookery and household management, therefore included a lot of Indian recipes in her book. It came as a real surprise to me to find that she was only twenty-nine when she died, yet her output had been phenomenal and she has become an enduring part of British cookery.

KALLEAH YEKHUNEE

Ingredients. – 2 lbs of the lean of mutton, 4 onions, $\frac{1}{2}$ oz each of ginger and cloves, 1 tbsp of sugar, 2 of lime juice, 1 dessert-spoonful of curry powder, salt and cayenne to taste, water. Mode. – Slice the meat into a stewpan with enough water to cover, add the seasoning and stew until the meat is tender. Strain off the gravy into another saucepan, mix together the sugar, lime-juice and curry powder with a little water, mix this with the gravy, pour it back on the meat and stew all for another 15 minutes.

Desperate Dan

What can I say about Desperate Dan! Every school child who has read of his antics over the last 50 years in the *Dandy* knows as much as I do. I have always been a fan of Dan's and his straightforward method of dealing with difficulties by walking right over them. I was delighted when he agreed to give me his recipe for Cow Pie but have to confess that it has not been tested in my own kitchen.

DESPERATE DAN'S COW-PIE

Take one cow, polish horns, launder tail and place in large pie dish. Dish should be first rubbed thoroughly with grizzly-bear grease and bear returned carefully to its cave. *Pastry* – Empty three sacks of flour into a cement mixer. Add six ostrich eggs and a horse-trough of water. Mix thoroughly. Roll out pastry with road roller, driven carefully at 3 mph. [Cover cow with pastry.] Garnish with a pint of owlhoot juice (Spare pastry can be kept for multifarious uses, such as filling pot-holes in the road.) Bake in a moderately hot volcano till crust turns a golden black! May be served with granite chips and fresh cactus shoots. Essence of polecat will add a certain piquancy to gravy. Season to taste – or take with a large pinch of salt!

Serves five large families or one Desperate Dan
© Aunt Minnie

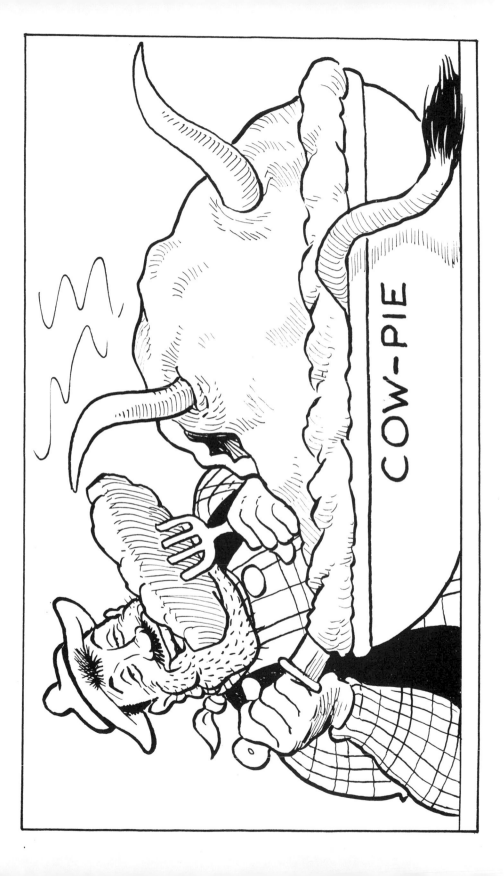

A Delicate Disposition

Richard Kirwan was yet another eighteenth-century eccentric who had an independent income and organized brilliant soirées – provided you arrived by 7 and left promptly two hours later. He always ate alone, and only ever had a dish of ham and milk. He was of a delicate disposition, which was perhaps an excuse for his preambulatory routine. He would 'accumulate' maximum heat from an open fire by standing in front of it with his coat open, quickly fasten the coat, don a hat, and walk briskly about outside, not speaking a word to passers-by or removing his hat in case the heat escaped. He wouldn't go to church for the same reason, and he may have been right if the old saying of losing most of our body-heat through the tops of our heads is true! (Unfortunately, he died through starving himself to death!)

BACHELOR'S HAM PIE

$\frac{1}{2}$ lb ham, cut up, 3 pints of flour, 3 tablespoonfuls of cream of tartar, $\frac{1}{2}$ cup of butter, $1\frac{1}{2}$ teaspoonfuls of carbonate of soda, and milk. Cut up the ham, put it into a stewpan with enough water to make the gravy; it will only be necessary to let it come to a boil; season it. Make a crust with the flour, &c., dissolving the soda first in hot water, and rubbing the cream of tartar into the butter. Add sufficient milk to make a stiff paste, then roll it out, butter the sides of a deep earthen baking-dish, and line them with paste, but leave the bottom untouched. Put in the pie funnel, thicken the gravy with a little flour, pour it over the ham, put on the top crust, and bake three quarters of an hour.

Here is a recipe suitable for one of Frank Buckland's Society for the Acclimatization of Animals dinners.

CURRIED KANGAROO TAILS

The tail and tongue are the only parts of the animal that are eaten.
Ingredients: Fresh onions, butter, any cold vegetables (the greater the variety the better), curry powder, gravy, rice, jointed kangaroo tail which has been stewed like an ox-tail for about an hour, or the tongue, likewise stewed. Mode: Slice the onions, and fry them brown in butter, mix the curry powder to a paste with a little gravy, stir in, and afterwards the kangaroo meat as used. Simmer in the fying pan until well mixed, then add the vegetables chopped fine and simmer further. Serve with boiled rice.

Fred Dibnah

Being eccentric doesn't necessarily mean that your taste in food is exotic.

I first came across the renowned steeplejack Fred Dibnah when he was buying his Bolton house and was impressed by his head for heights. I only wish I had felt so insouciant when I was circling Weston Park strapped to the roof of a small biplane. Apparently Fred has his feet firmly on the ground when it comes to food, eating chips at home and corned beef hash at work.

CORNED BEEF HASH

$\frac{1}{2}$ lb corned beef
1 medium boiled onion
Worcester sauce
2 tbsp flour

4 medium boiled potatoes
$\frac{1}{2}$ green pepper
2 oz butter
$\frac{1}{4}$ pint stock

Dice the corned beef, potatoes and onion. Remove the seeds from the pepper and chop it. Melt the butter, add the flour and cook for a few minutes. Add the stock slowly, and heat until boiling and the sauce thickens. Add the meat and vegetables and mix. Then fry in a little fat until the underneath is crisp and brown.

The Experimenter

The Honourable Henry Cavendish finds his rightful place here as eccentric, philosopher and experimenter – enormously wealthy and very, very shy. He lived with his father in Clapham until he was fifty-two, which may perhaps explain both his wealth and his shyness. Somehow he managed to overcome the latter to become a noted member of the Royal Society. He was, however, permitted to attend their dinners with only a five-shilling allowance for the meal. His renown as an experimenter came largely through his demonstration of the composition of water and every room in his house was converted for scientific experiments.

Cavendish could not bear to be spoken to directly, took absolutely no interest in being the largest stock-holder in the Bank of England, and always dined on a leg of mutton. Even when he entertained, the meal was a leg of mutton, increased to two if the number of guests warranted it.

BOILED MUTTON WITH DUMPLINGS AND CAPER SAUCE

1 3–4 lb leg of mutton
1 large turnip
3 medium onions
2 tsp chopped parsley

1 tsp salt
3 medium carrots
2 tbsp pearl barley

Boil enough water to cover the meat, put in the meat best side down. Bring again to the boil, skim, add the vegetables cut in medium sized pieces and the salt. Lower the heat and simmer for nearly 2 hours for a 4 lb joint, 20 minutes less for a 3 lb joint. Garnish with chopped parsley over the joint and the vegetables round the dish.

TO FORCE A LEG OF MUTTON

Raise the skin and take out the lean part of the mutton, chop it exceeding fine, with one anchovy, shred a bundle of sweet herbs, grate a penny loaf, half a lemon, nutmeg, pepper, and salt to your taste, make them into a forcemeat, with three eggs and a large glass of red wine, fill up the skin with the forcemeat, but leave the bone and shank in their place, and it will appear like a whole leg, lay it on an earthen dish with a pint of red wine under it, and send it to the oven; it will take two hours and a half; when it comes out take off all the fat, strain the gravy over the mutton, lay round it hard yolks of eggs and pickled mushrooms: garnish with pickles, and serve it up.

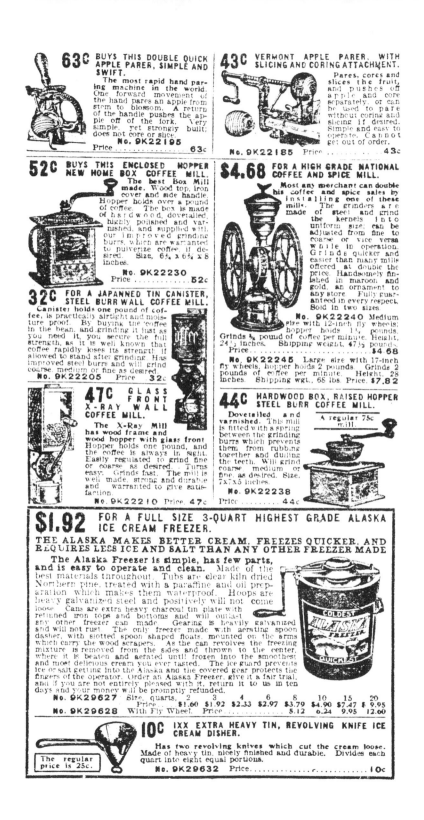

63c BUYS THIS DOUBLE QUICK APPLE PARER, SIMPLE AND SWIFT.

The most rapid hand paring machine in the world. One forward movement of the hand pares an apple from stem to blossom. A return of the handle pushes the apple off of the fork. Very simple, yet strongly built; does not core or slice.
No. 9K22195
Price 63c

43c VERMONT APPLE PARER, WITH SLICING AND CORING ATTACHMENT.

Pares, cores and slices the fruit, and pushes off apple and core separately, or can be used to pare without coring and slicing if desired. Simple and easy to operate. Cannot get out of order.
No. 9K22185   Price 43c

52c BUYS THIS ENCLOSED HOPPER NEW HOME BOX COFFEE MILL.

The best Box Mill made. Wood top, iron cover and side handle. Hopper holds over a pound of coffee. The box is made of hardwood, dovetailed, highly polished and varnished, and supplied with our improved grinding burrs, which are warranted to pulverize coffee if desired. Size, 6¼ x 6¼ x 8 inches.
No. 9K22230
Price 52c

$4.68 FOR A HIGH GRADE NATIONAL COFFEE AND SPICE MILL.

Most any merchant can double his coffee and spice sales by installing one of these mills. The grinders are made of steel and grind the kernels into uniform size; can be adjusted from fine to coarse or vice versa while in operation. Grinds quicker and easier than many mills offered at double the price. Handsomely finished in maroon and gold, an ornament to any store. Fully guaranteed in every respect. Sold in two sizes.
No. 9K22240 Medium size with 12-inch fly wheels; hopper holds 1¼ pounds. Grinds ¾ pound of coffee per minute. Height, 24½ inches. Shipping weight, 47½ pounds.
Price $4.68
No. 9K22245 Large size with 17-inch fly wheels, hopper holds 2 pounds. Grinds 2 pounds of coffee per minute. Height, 28 inches. Shipping wgt., 68 lbs. Price, $7.82

32c FOR A JAPANNED TIN CANISTER, STEEL BURR WALL COFFEE MILL.

Canister holds one pound of coffee, is practically airtight and moisture proof. By buying the coffee in the bean, and grinding it just as you need it, you secure the full strength, as it is well known that coffee rapidly loses its strength if allowed to stand after grinding. Has improved steel burrs and will grind coarse, medium or fine as desired.
No. 9K22205   Price 32c

47c GLASS FRONT X-RAY WALL COFFEE MILL.

The X-Ray Mill has wood frame and wood hopper with glass front. Hopper holds one pound, and the coffee is always in sight. Easily regulated to grind fine or coarse as desired. Turns easy. Grinds fast. The mill is well made, strong and durable and warranted to give satisfaction.
No. 9K22210 Price, 47c

44c HARDWOOD BOX, RAISED HOPPER STEEL BURR COFFEE MILL.

A regular 75c mill.

Dovetailed and varnished. This mill is fitted with a spring between the grinding burrs which prevents them from rubbing together and dulling the teeth. Will grind coarse, medium or fine, as desired. Size, 7x7x5 inches.
No. 9K22238
Price 44c

$1.92 FOR A FULL SIZE 3-QUART HIGHEST GRADE ALASKA ICE CREAM FREEZER.

THE ALASKA MAKES BETTER CREAM, FREEZES QUICKER, AND REQUIRES LESS ICE AND SALT THAN ANY OTHER FREEZER MADE

The Alaska Freezer is simple, has few parts, and is easy to operate and clean. Made of the best materials throughout. Tubs are clear kiln dried Northern pine, treated with a paraffine and oil preparation which makes them waterproof. Hoops are heavy galvanized steel and positively will not come loose. Cans are extra heavy charcoal tin plate with retinned iron tops and bottoms and will outlast any other freezer can made. Gearing is heavily galvanized and will not rust. The only freezer made with aerating spoon dasher, with slotted spoon shaped floats, mounted on the arms which carry the wood scrapers. As the can revolves the freezing mixture is removed from the sides and thrown to the center, where it is beaten and aerated until frozen into the smoothest and most delicious cream you ever tasted. The ice guard prevents ice or salt getting into the Alaska and the covered gear protects the fingers of the operator. Order an Alaska Freezer, give it a fair trial, and if you are not entirely pleased with it, return it to us in ten days and your money will be promptly refunded.

No. 9K29627 Size, quarts,	2	3	4	6	8	10	15	20
Price	$1.60	$1.92	$2.33	$2.97	$3.79	$4.90	$7.47	$9.95
No. 9K29628 With Fly Wheel. Price....			5.12	6.24		9.95		12.60

10c IXX EXTRA HEAVY TIN, REVOLVING KNIFE ICE CREAM DISHER.

The regular price is 25c.

Has two revolving knives which cut the cream loose. Made of heavy tin, nicely finished and durable. Divides each quart into eight equal portions.
No. 9K29632   Price........................ 10c

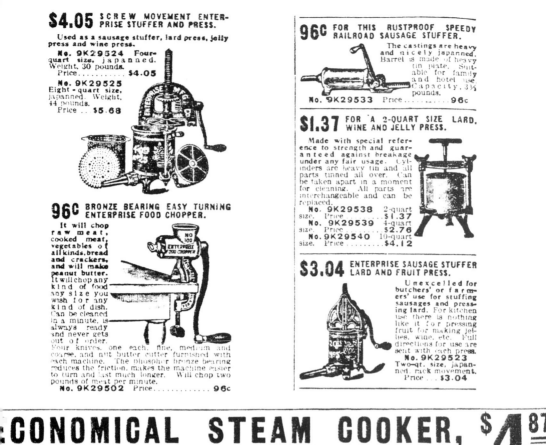
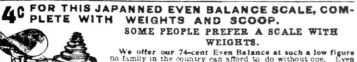

Prince of the Holy Roman Empire

The Rev. Mr Egerton is another of that amusing band of eighteenth-century eccentrics – who in fact carried on into the nineteenth century! His father was the Bishop of Durham and when Francis became the 8th Earl of Bridgewater in 1823 with an income of £40,000 a year he was at last able to display visibly his pride in the family name. He marked everything possible with the Bridgewater coat of arms – dog collars included. Despite this particular flamboyance, he lived quietly (albeit in fine aristocratic style), most frequently dining alone with his dogs. A self-styled Prince of the Holy Roman Empire, Egerton spent much of his life in Paris, speaking Latin because he never learned French, and conducting small-scale hunts in his gardens, complete with pink coats and specially imported fox and hounds.

I am not quite sure why the period produced so many memorable personalities with unconventional lives, but it must have been a most interesting time to be around. Here is the recipe for Egerton's favourite dish, most often prepared for him by his chef, Viard.

BOILED BEEF AND POTATOES

Silverside is best for this recipe.

Tie the beef round with string. Bring to the boil a large pan of water and add peeled and chopped potatoes, parsnips and a few sticks of celery. When the water has come to the boil again, add the beef and cover the pan. Then move the saucepan until it is only half on the fire, or lower the heat, so that the water just simmers. After about 20 minutes, remove any scum from the broth. Add whole black peppercorns and some spice. Recover and simmer until the meat is tender and the vegetables cooked. Drain and serve the meat and vegetables separately on hot dishes, using the broth (thickened a little with arrowroot) as gravy.

Not a Gentleman's Gentleman

There are as many female eccentrics as male ones. Charlotte Cibber failed at everything – including dressing as a man, because in this guise she had the misfortune to have a very rich young woman fall hopelessly in love with her and she was forced to take up valeting to escape her attentions. Char-

lotte was bankrupted twice, despite trying the widest possible variety of jobs. She was by turn, among other things, an actress, grocer, inn-keeper and sausage-maker.

A COUNTRY WAY TO MAKE SAUSAGES

Take pork, not so much fat as lean, mince it exceeding small together, then take part of the *fleck* of pork, which is the suet, in pieces about the bigness of the top of your finger, season each apart with minced sage, good store of pe, per and salt, some cloves and mace; mix in the seasoning into each of them; take the small sheep's guts and cleanse them (others use capon's guts) and fill them with your funnel, always putting some of the fleck between the minced. If you have it ready you may sprinkle a little *sack* on the top of the sausage meat, it will make it fill the better.

These are a few recipes found by that venturesome breed – anthropologists – in their travels around the world. I was fascinated to read them and to add them to my collection.

The first is Faroese and demonstrates that old adage, 'Waste not, want not'.

BOILED SHEEP'S HEAD

Burn the wool off the head with a flame. Saw the head in two longitudinally between the eyes. Put the halves in a saucepan with boiling water, add salt and herbs and peppercorns to taste. Simmer for about 2 hours until the meat slips away from the bone. Allow half a head per person. Serve with boiled potatoes and melted butter. Place the heads on a plate in the centre of the table where everyone can reach and pick or cut off what they want. Everything can be eaten except the bones. Fastidious persons may omit the eyeballs and the gums.

The next 'recipe' comes from Isobel White, who relates this story about her experiences in the outback in *The Anthropologists' Cookbook*.

The Whistling Steak

A fact discovered by the Aborigines, and useful to people who are hard-pressed for food, is that food soaked in water loses any poisonous content (as witness the treatment of cycad palm nuts). Anything that has 'gone off' is soaked by the Aborigines.

I remember a 10 lb piece of rump steak that was hanging so long that it swelled up and went perfectly green. In fact, it whistled when you passed it. I yelled out to one of the people to throw it away. He said, 'No, we'll take it to the camp and eat it. This is good tucker.'

This is what the locals did: they soaked that piece of steak for two days in running water, then they cooked it in the ground oven with leaves around it, as usual, to flavour it. After it was cooked and taken out, it looked so beautiful and smelled so good that I reckoned I would have a little bit of it. It was absolutely marvellous! It was tender and tasty, and provided that you could get over the fact that it had been green, it made a fine meal.

A veterinary friend later told me that it was quite safe to have eaten the 'whistling steak'. The bacilli that poison people, he said, are on the meat only when it *first* starts to go off. Once meat goes green *it is not poisonous*. The water and the fire destroyed both the bacilli and the smell.

Finally in this trio, Ropa Vieja. Don't be put off by the English translation – Old Clothes. It is a Panamanian recipe which is now something of a rarity in the countryside, but used to be cooked for wedding parties or to celebrate the building of a house.

ROPA VIEJA

1 lb chuck or stewing steak
pepper and salt to taste
1 clove garlic
1 tbsp Worcestershire sauce

$\frac{1}{4}$ cup water
$\frac{1}{4}$ cup vinegar
$2\frac{1}{2}$ tsp soy sauce
1 finely chopped medium onion

Sprinkle the raw meat lightly with salt and pepper, then place in a flat shallow dish with vinegar and soak for 2–3 hours. Place the soaked meat in a pot with an inch or so of water and simmer for 15–30 minutes. Remove and chop it into small, thin strips, and place in a frying-pan with the onion, salt and pepper and garlic. Mix together the water, soy sauce and Worcestershire sauce and add to the meat. Simmer slowly until almost all the moisture evaporates. The result is a tasty meat coated with a thin sauce. As a variation, a little tomato paste may be added to the sauce.

Quick-cooking, corrupted, variation

If a more tender cut of meat is used, such as round steak, brown the meat and onions quickly in 2 tbsp cooking oil, then add the sauce and boil until the moisture almost evaporates. To prepare the sauce, mix 2 tsp vinegar, 2 tsp soy sauce, 1 tbsp Worcestershire sauce and 2 tbsp tomato sauce.

April Ashley

April is a most beautiful woman even though she is now of 'a certain age'. She was born a boy, in Liverpool, and was the youngest of six children. For a while she was a merchant seaman. Yet she always felt destined to be a woman. She of course achieved fame and a high society life after her sex-change in the 1960s, but has given all that up for a much quieter life. Despite everything April has certainly got style, and a style which has been recognized by a wide variety of people, including Salvador Dali, as she told me when giving me the next recipe.

'The most eccentric dinner I ever had was with a cousin of Salvador Dali. This came about because Dali wished very much to paint me as Hermaphradite, but as I was in my early twenties and still in my halfway house so to speak, I just did not have the courage to pose. But during these meetings (in Paris) his cousin invited me to dinner (more pressure). He gave me a wonderful spaghetti bolon but instead of Parmesan cheese he used tin tacks. Well, as I said, the spaghetti was delicious – but it was exhausting spitting out the tacks.

'My own favourite recipe is most ironic as I am a complete salt freak. My ex-husband (Lord Rowallan) used to say I was the only person he'd ever seen put salt on anchovies. Well, for this recipe you need no salt, pepper or other seasoning as it is all in the ingredients. In fact you will need one hell of a lot of wine and mineral water on the table.'

APRIL ASHLEY'S SIRLOIN STEAK WITH OYSTERS

Sirloin steak
Smoked oysters
Jar of small gherkins
Onion
Oyster sauce

Rice
Lots of vegetables and salad
Soy sauce

Cut the steak very thin but as large as a long playing record. Lay it out, put a row of smoked oysters across its width. Cut the gherkins and onion into thin strips and place them with the oysters. Roll the steak up and put a cocktail stick at each end to keep the roll intact. Place in a casserole dish and cover with oyster sauce. Pour a few drops of soy sauce over each steak and cook in a pre-heated oven at 450° F for 45 minutes. Serve on a bed of rice with lots of quick fried veg and lots of green salad with lemon dressing.

57

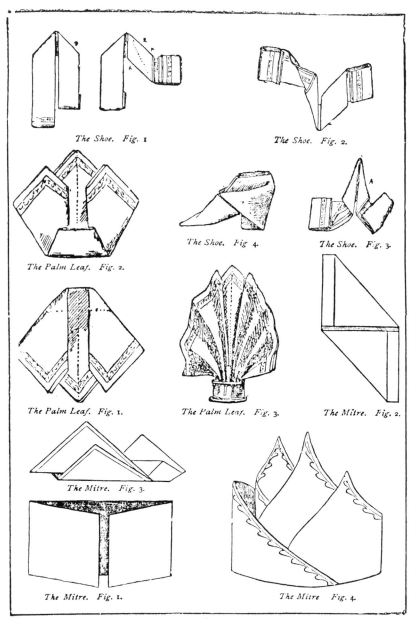

The Shoe. Fig. 1

The Shoe. Fig. 2.

The Palm Leaf. Fig. 2.

The Shoe. Fig 4.

The Shoe. Fig. 3.

The Palm Leaf. Fig. 1.

The Palm Leaf. Fig. 3.

The Mitre. Fig. 2.

The Mitre. Fig. 3.

The Mitre. Fig. 1.

The Mitre Fig. 4.

Serviettes.

3088.—DINNER FOR TWELVE PERSONS.—FEBRUARY.

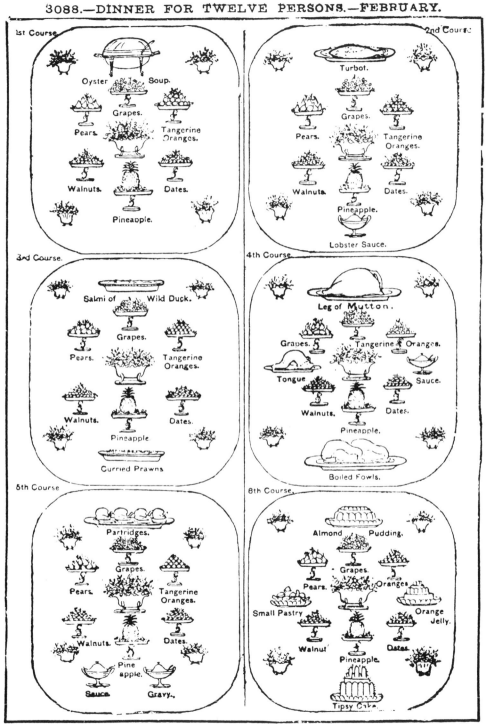

Note.—According to the size of the table, it might be as well to omit putting on the dessert till after the sixth course

RAM GOAT LIVER

According to this traditional Jamaican calypso-cum-recipe the liver of the ram goat is far and away the most effective portion. Every country has different ideas about what sort of food has aphrodisiac qualities, and whoever wrote this calypso was convinced that there was nothing to beat the aphrodisiac effect of ram goat liver. Take heed of the moral in the last verse!

Sunday gone I jump on a minibus
I really late but is not my faul'
And when we nearly reach by de terminus
I feel de bus come to a halt
We lick a ram goat down by de roundabout
But jus' as if dat could not suffice
A bredder run to de bus and start to shout
'He should a dead – mek we buy a pound a rice.'

Chorus: *Ram goat liver good fe mek mannish water,*
  Billy goat teet' mek de errings in your dahter,
  Curry goat lunch put de bite in your bark,
  It mek your dahter . . . it mek your dahter walk and talk.

Well de news spread fas' like a telegram
Nobody know where de goat come from
We raise a pot and a pan from an iyah'-man
Who sid down dere all a-long
Two twos and de pot a'bwile,
A head of yam and banana bake,
Meanwhile lickle waters a-gwan
Lick me goat and I tek me sip

Well I start to belch and I mek a sigh
I tek a walk for out de street
But while I wait down de road fe bum a ride
I feel a gripe and I start to feel very weak
Before too long you no haf fe ask –
I runnin' belly like a judgment day
Ah everybody in de road a-dead wid laugh
Is den I know dat crime will never pay.

Edward Fox

Edward Fox is a wonderfully talented actor, eccentric in a very understated English way. His Englishness is carried into the type of food he likes – 'very good, interesting sausages, brilliantly-understood mashed potatoes and home-made chutney' suit him a treat any time. 'Failing that, steak and kidney pie as only English country women can make it, is just as good.'

ENGLISH STEAK AND KIDNEY PIE

Shortcrust pastry to cover flat-edged pie dish – put in fridge when made

$1\frac{1}{2}$ lbs best braising steak	$\frac{1}{2}$ of a beef kidney
2 medium onions	Dripping
3 tbsp flour	Salt & black pepper

Cut the beef into cubes. De-vein kidney and cut into small pieces. Dust all the meat with seasoned flour. Slice the onions. Heat dripping in a frying pan and very gently fry the steak, kidney and onions for about half an hour. Add seasoning and stock or water to make a thick gravy. Pour into a saucepan, cover and simmer for $1\frac{1}{2}$ hours. Pour into a pie dish, and place a pie funnel in the middle. Leave to cool. Meanwhile, roll out pastry to be able to cut 1 inch strips to cover the rim of the wetted pie dish, then cover the whole dish – you will have a double crust at the edge of the pie dish. Make a cut over the pie funnel. Decorate crust with any remaining pastry and 'cut up' the edge of the crust horizontally with a knife, and crimp. Wash the crust lightly with beaten egg, and bake at 350° F until golden brown.

An Experienced Housekeeper

I love Elizabeth Raffald's cookery book, which has a delightfully straightforward attitude to cooking. What else would we expect from the lady who organized the first Midwives' Guild? Many of the recipes in her bestseller, *The Experienced English Housekeeper* (which went into thirteen editions), appeal to me as much for their strange names as anything else. How about this one?

TO MAKE A PORCUPINE OF A BREAST OF VEAL

Bone the finest and largest breast of veal you can get, rub it over with the yolks of two eggs, spread it on a table, lay over it a little bacon cut as thin as possible, a handful of parsley shred fine, the yolks of five hard boiled eggs chopped small, a little lemon peel cut fine, nutmeg, pepper, and salt to your taste, and the crumb of a penny loaf steeped in cream, roll the breast close, and skewer it up, then cut fat bacon and the lean of ham that has been a little boiled, or it will turn the veal red, and pickled cucumbers about two inches long to answer the other lardings, and lard it in rows, first ham, then bacon, then cucumbers, till you have larded it all over the veal; put it in a deep earthen pot, with a pint of water, and cover it and set it in a slow oven two hours; when it comes from the oven skim the fat off, and strain the gravy through a sieve into a stew-pan, put in a glass of white wine, a little lemon pickle and caper liquor, a spoonful of mushroom catch-up, thicken it with a little butter, rolled in flour, lay your porcupine on the dish, and pour it hot upon it, cut a roll of forcemeat in four slices, lay one at each end and the other at the sides; have ready your sweetbread cut in slices and fried, lay them round it with a few mushrooms. It is a grand bottom dish when game is not to be had.

N.B. Make the forcemeat of a few chopped oysters, the crumbs of a penny loaf, half a pound of beef suet shred fine, and the yolks of four eggs, mix them well together with nutmeg, Chyan pepper, and salt to your palate, spread it on a veal caul, and roll it up close like a collared eel, bind it in a cloth and boil it one hour.

The EXPERIENCED

Englifh Houfe-keeper,

For the Ufe and Eafe of

Ladies, Houfe-keepers, Cooks, &c.

Wrote purely from PRACTICE,

Eliz: And dedicated to the *Raffald*

Hon. Lady ELIZABETH WARBURTON,

Whom the Author lately ferved as Houfe-keeper.

Confifting of near 800 Original Receipts, moft of which never appeared in Print.

PART FIRST, Lemon Pickle, Browning, for all Sorts of Made Difhes, Soups, Fifh, plain Meat, Game, Made Difhes both hot and cold, Pyes, Puddings, &c,

PART SECOND, All Kind of Confectionary, particularly the Gold and Silver Web for covering of Sweetmeats, and a Defert of Spun Sugar, with Directions to fet out a Table in the moft elegant Manner and in the modern Tafte, Floating Iflands, Fifh Ponds, Tranfparent Puddings, Trifles, Whips, &c.

PART THIRD, Pickling, Potting, and Collaring, Wines, Vinegars, Catchups, Diftilling, with two moft valuable Receipts, one for refining Malt Liquors, the other for curing Acid Wines, and a correct Lift of every Thing in Seafon in every Month of the Year.

By ELIZABETH RAFFALD.

MANCHESTER:

Printed by *J. Harrop*, for the Author, and fold by Meffrs. *Fletcher* and *Anderfon*, in *St. Paul's* Church-yard, *London*; and by *Eliz. Raffald*, Confectioner, near the *Exchange, Manchefter*, 1769.

The Book to be figned by the Author's own Hand-writing, and entered at Stationers Hall.

Another Experienced Housekeeper

This comes from the original edition of Mrs Beeton. Mrs Beeton did not shirk anything in her determination to make her book on cookery and household management totally comprehensive as her Roast Wallaby recipe shows.

64 .

ROAST WALLABY

Ingredients. – Wallaby, forcemeat, milk, butter.
Mode. – In winter the animal may hang for some days, as a hare, which it resembles, but in summer it must, like all other flesh, be cooked very soon after it is killed. Cut off the hind-legs at the first joints, and, after skinning and paunching, let it lie in water for a little while to draw out the blood. Make a good veal forcemeat, and after well washing the inside of the wallaby, stuff it and sew it up. Truss as a hare and roast before a bright clear fire from $1\frac{1}{4}$ to $1\frac{3}{4}$ hour, according to size. It must be kept some distance from the fire when first put down, or the outside will be too dry before the inside is done. Baste well, first with milk and then with butter, and when nearly done dredge with flour and baste again with butter till nicely frothed.
Time – $1\frac{1}{4}$ to $1\frac{3}{4}$ hour.
Sufficient for 6 persons.
Seasonable – best in cold weather.

Jimmy Savile, OBE

Jimmy Savile has had a most extraordinary career. Son of a miner, he now hobnobs with the most influential people in the land. His main claim to fame is that he has raised over £10 million for Stoke Mandeville Hospital. Nobody knows much about Jimmy Savile's lifestyle, although apart from some expensive cars he seems to keep it all remarkably simple. He is very keen on running, often for charity, but is clearly no health fanatic if this recipe is anything to go by!

MILLIONAIRE'S MUNCH

1 tin of tomato soup
1 tin of beans
1 tin of anything of your choice [such as mince]

Place these in the pan. Heat. Eat straight from pan. Do not burn yourself on hot pan.

(Live like this and you too can be rich in a year.)

Norman Parkinson

Parkinson is the society photographer who manages to make everybody look beautiful. His photographs have a misty, fragile quality which is immensely flattering. He has been so successful that he and his wife are able to live for the greater part of the year in Tobago. Like all expatriates, he seems to hanker after the simplest of English dishes, in this case a version of bangers and mash.

'Porkinson Pottage is a dish (or occasion) that I can only organize while staying in the UK where I have a small flat and a smaller kitchen.

'British Television is far and away the most entertaining in the world. Both the best and the worst are absolutely first class . . .

'Television, being highly soporific, should always be watched in bed.'

Hence the invention of the Porkinson Pottage, a one saucepan delight.'

PORKINSON POTTAGE

Take down a medium size pan, cover with water 2 or 3 medium sized potatoes either peeled or scrubbed, depending how tired you feel, throw in a walnut of sea salt. When spuds start to boil throw in three or four of your absolute favourite bangers (pork sausages) terribly difficult today to find a really good variety but search and search. When the spuds are almost cooked (use fork) hook out the bangers now done (this can be during the commercials) and keep them warm nearby. Throw into the boiling spuds a fistful of prepared cabbage and a scratch of nutmeg. Return at the next commercial break, drain water, and bash up with a mash plunger the $\frac{1}{2}$-cooked cabbage with the now soft spuds. Here use a lump of butter and pepper mill (keep it all moving). Sometimes I drop an egg in, sometimes a few grates of cheddar or parmesan, whatever I find in the bachelor fridge (the loneliest place in the world). Hey presto! This triumph of Escoffier is now complete – pop back the warm sausages in the warm pan. A smear of Colmans. Turn off the stove, seize a napkin, fork and spoon. Jump back into bed holding saucepan handle, place napkin on belly, place warm pan on belly (tremendous comfort) and eat the 'mess of pottage' without averting lunatic gaze from idiot box. Warning, when you place empty saucepan by your bed with meal completed avoid anticipated area where you might put foot out later, to make three am journey to evacuate liquid excesses. A half asleep foot in a saucepan at this time can make you unpopular with your neighbours.

Tom Gilbey

I have known the colourful Tom Gilbey for about fifteen years – we probably met at a London party or two, although I don't remember exactly how this came about, except that we were both young dogs in those days!

Very few British designers rise to the top of the fashion scene and stay there – Tom Gilbey has accomplished this with originality and style and is one of our foremost designers. If you remember safari suits and flares and polo-neck sweaters for men, you were influenced by Tom Gilbey. And if, today, you are favouring more informal wear for your business lunches, you are still influenced by Tom Gilbey.

I am delighted that he found the time to give me this recipe for a truly well-proportioned potato, and its filling!

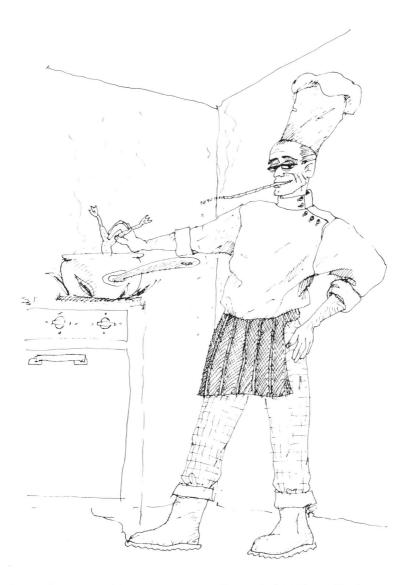

GILBEY'S JUMPING JACKET TAILOR MADE TO ORDER

Ingredients

Well proportioned potato
Succulent, freshly obtained frogs' legs
Beluga caviar
Lemon
Newly acquired truffles
and of course, don't forget the butter.

Method

First . . . approach your local 'Home Grown' supplier, who should also be legitimizing his window box by growing a few reds!

Frogs' legs . . . having obtained your tattie and hopefully having recovered from the previous night's straight . . . you should arise early, at 4.00 am to be exact, suitably attired in Hunters, wet suit and Husky (which you doubtless will be later). Landing net grasped firmly in hand and thunderflash well concealed, take yourself off to country parts – ignoring the stunned looks of sleepy milkmen etc. Upon reaching a suitable spot, go slithering off into the undergrowth in search of a succulent, dew covered, virgin frog. Use whatever method you deem best to snare this beast, but I firmly suggest the thunderflash and the net. Stun 'em and scoop 'em up. However, if your imagination can improve on this method, please write to me c/o Box No. 333

Truffles . . . you will be pleased to know that these can now be found in London. Sniff yourself around Fortnum's Food Hall, constantly on the lookout for men in red jackets . . . who may regard you with suspicion – PAY NO ATTENTION – SNIFF ON.

Beluga . . . having more than likely been thrown out of Piccadilly's finest store, best repair to your residence and dispatch your man to Harrod's to pick up a jar of caviar. Do something difficult, such as having a Bucks Fizz until he returns.

Lemon . . . all that crawling around in damp circumstances will doubtless have left you with at least a chill, though more likely double pneumonia; so pluck and squeeze one for a health giving drink, but save just a sliver for the garnish.

Bake potato – sauté, boil, fricassee or poach the rest of the ingredients in any way you wish, but PLEASE arrange aesthetically.

Bon appetit!

Oh! and don't forget the butter.

FISH DISHES

Dame Hilda Bracket

I am a devoted fan of Dame Hilda Bracket and suspect that we probably share a common ancestry somewhere along the line, as she is one of the Brackets of Bracket Towers – a charmingly eccentric aristocratic pile hidden somewhere in the depths of the Kentish countryside. I am so pleased that since Dame Hilda moved to Stackton Tressle we are now near neighbours. Naturally Dame Hilda was delighted to let me add one of her favourite recipes to my collection and was kind enough to fill me in on the background in her own inimitable style, which I think is sometimes known as 'train of consciousness'.

'This dish was created to celebrate the re-stringing of Dr Hinge's banjo. In her student days Dr Hinge had earned extra money by playing the banjo, first house at the Glasgow Empire. (She wasn't brave enough to attempt the second house). She was of course a fellow of the University of Ord. Sadly now defunct. She had, she tells me, by now become what can only be described by some as a natural follow-up to the late George Formby. Had he ever known he probably wouldn't have died when he did. However, on a trip to the Festival of Britain, while poring over some early relics in the Dome of Discovery, where she had gone for a quiet glimpse into the past, some miscreant crept up behind her and winkled the mother of pearl inlay out of the neck of her instrument. (It is a long-necked tenor banjo). Similar to the one Lilian Bayliss used to play on the sands!

INCONSOLABLE

Needless to say, when she discovered what had happened she was inconsolable, and what made it worse she was on her way to a performance by the great man himself at the Palace Theatre in London. (Hoping, I suppose, to be asked to join him on stage). Things were never the same after this. In 1955 we went on a tour of Cyprus to entertain the troops, and I must say they were very appreciative. And it was on this trip that Evadne lost her precious stringed companion. Up till then it had never left her side. Everyone joined in the search and eventually it was located in an aeroplane hangar behind some oil drums. Without the strings and looking very sad. Not as sad as Evadne looked. Well, the happy pair were re-united and as a treat I created the special dish for my friend when we had all clubbed together and bought new strings. Needless to say she is now very careful where she takes it and even more careful where she leaves it – only once in the ladies' cloakroom at the Ritz.'

DAME HILDA BRACKET'S COD AUDETTE

Two fish steaks
  (cod/halibut/hake or
  similar)
Two prunes
For the marinade: dry white
  wine, 1 tbsp tarragon
  vinegar, 1 tsp caster sugar

bay leaves, juniper berries,
tarragon, salt and black
pepper

Soak the fish for several hours in the marinade before cooking.
Remove fish from marinade and take out any large bones that
appear, lay the fish on foil, add two bay leaves, two juniper
berries, a sprinkle of tarragon and fresh ground pepper. Place a
prune, preferably precooked or tinned in a suitable position on
top of each steak. Make the foil into a parcel and place in a
fire-proof dish in the centre of a medium oven adding a little
water in the base of the dish. Bake for 20 minutes or until
ready. Remove, and having thickened the marinade with
arrowroot* into a hot, pouring sauce, pour this over the fish.
Decorate with cucumber twists and serve with pommes frites or
sauté potatoes and broccoli. Serve on plain white china. And if
there is any wine left in the bottle, drink it with the meal. A
glass or two wouldn't really go amiss. Cheers!

*Alternative and richer thickening . . . 2 egg yolks and ½ gill of cream.

COCONUT LEAF COOKERY

Dame Hilda, who is mistress of the amusing anecdote, would appreciate this delightful tale. In response to an American company's survey on tourism in the Fijian islands, and their conclusion that more local food should be served, the *Fiji Times* wrote as follows:

The American advisers to the tourist trade have told us to offer people 'fish baked in coconut leaves'. This is an excellent dish (says an experimental cook) which is too seldom seen on our tables. One fish and two coconut leaves will be enough. There is no difficulty about the fish; but the leaves will require careful manipulation. It is not so much getting them into the oven as getting them to the kitchen. Those who lead with the feeble or wavy end of the leaf mostly fail. You should take the *thick* end – the part that was joined to the tree – clasp it tightly to your waist, and run smartly into the kitchen. The thin end follows, as do various ornaments, side-tables, and teacups collected on the way. The second leaf, however, will have a clear field of entry. Take the fish, and wrap the leaves carefully around it in all directions. Most fish seem to resent this and tend to slither away. A good plan is to take eight broomsticks, and stack them in the kitchen like bivouacked rifles, then the fish can be firmly wedged on top, and the wrapping undertaken with free hands. You should start wrapping *always* with the *thin* end of each leaf so that most of the work will have been done when you come to the awful business of wrapping with the thick ends. Many people (writes Aunt Betsy) just forget about the last little inch or two, and leave them sticking out. Do not pause in the wrapping process, because coconut leaves are great unwrappers. When the fish is fully wrapped, you can tie the bundle with wire and carefully remove the broomsticks one by one. Then give the bundle a good *shake* in an *up-and-down* direction, when the fish will easily slide out and can be baked in a tin in the usual way.

Mackerel Kettle.

USTENSILES ET APPAREILS.

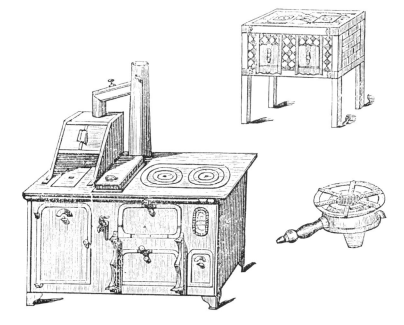

Fig. 1. F g. 2. A.

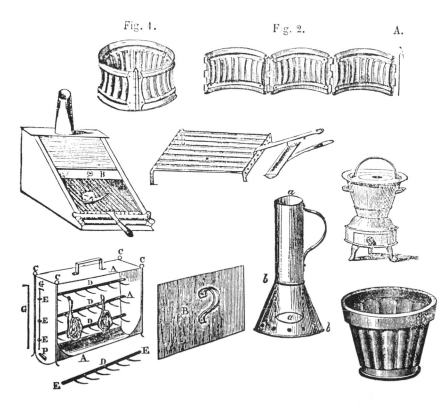

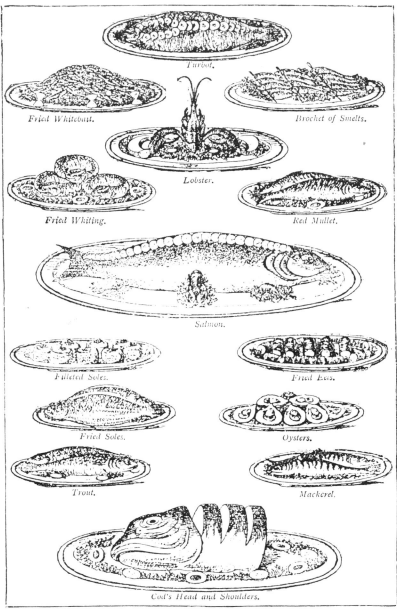

Turbot.

Fried Whitebait.

Brochet of Smelts.

Lobster.

Fried Whiting.

Red Mullet.

Salmon.

Filleted Soles.

Fried Eels.

Fried Soles.

Oysters.

Trout.

Mackerel.

Cod's Head and Shoulders.

Fish.

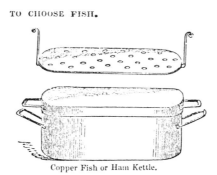

Copper Fish or Ham Kettle.

Bottom Heat

I came across this comment about Daniel Dancer recently: 'When he was obliged to relieve the wants of nature, he would rather walk two miles than not assist in manuring his own land.' And it proves not to be too extreme an example of Dancer's tightfistedness, which covered every aspect of his own life. At the other extreme, he was generous almost to a fault with friends.

Daniel Dancer was particularly mean when it came to food. He tried to make one piece of beef and dumplings last a week, so he never wasted an opportunity to get food free. He and his sister once dragged home a rotting sheep's carcass to make into mutton pies. He then accused her of using up the pies too quickly.

They were by no means poor – over £3,000 was found secreted away when Dancer died, yet he had been too mean to buy his own snuff, taking the offerings of others for his own snuff box; and too mean to call a doctor to his dying sister. A neighbour looked after him after his sister died, sending him a dish of trout in red wine. But Dancer was too mean to light a fire to heat the dish, so sat on it to warm it through. I wonder if he boiled the muslin cloth which would have covered such a dish for soup the following week?

A GOOD WAY TO STEW FISH

Mix half a tumbler of wine with as much water as will cover the fish in the stew-pan and put in a little pepper and salt, three or four onions, a crust of bread toasted very brown, one anchovy, a good lump of butter, and set them over a gentle fire, shake the stew-pan now and then that it may not burn; just before you serve it up, pour your gravy into a saucepan, and thicken it with a little butter rolled in flour, a little catchup and walnut pickle, beat well together till smooth, then pour it on your fish, and set it over the fire to heat, and serve it up hot.

I include this as yet another recipe which shows that Mrs Beeton was not daunted by any ingredient. The dish comes from India. First find your chilwars . . .

CHILWARS

Ingredients. – Fish, hot lard or clarified dripping, green limes, flour, salt. Mode. – These small silvery fish somewhat resemble whitebait, although a trifle larger. They are run on sticks, sprinkled with flour and a little salt, then fried in boiling lard as whitebait. They should be very crisp and dry. They are served with fresh cut green limes, instead of lemons as here, and are sent to table on the sticks, which are run through their heads, or, with greater elegance, strung upon a thin silver skewer.

3. doz. native Oysters for 10/- from Cowes.

WE GUARANTEE this Season's Medina Native Fattened OYSTERS to be the finest in the world, and are far superior to any others that are advertised at a low price, which CANNOT POSSIBLY be the GENUINE Medina or Whitstable Oysters; as, owing to the enormous trade done by us, we are able to send three dozen Native Oysters, in a wooden barrel, and Postage Paid to any part of the Kingdom for 10s., this being just the wholesale price, with only the cost of barrel and postage added, so we can defy anyone to sell them at a lower rate.

The Medina Oysters were sent on board of H.R.H. the Prince of Wales' Yacht, daily, whilst at Cowes this summer and to the Court at Osborne.

For further Particulars apply to THE COWES PARCELS POST NATIVE OYSTER SUPPLY ASSOCIATION, Medina-road, Cowes, I.W.

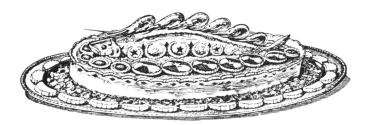

Steam Baths

Captain Thomas Gibson Bowles only ever took steam baths, considering it impossible to get clean by sitting in dirty water.

He had been widowed in 1887 and, with four children under ten and little time to attend to childish ailments, Cap'en Tommy decided to raise his children in the Jewish faith. He had done a little research and discovered that those living under Mosaic law had a greater resistance to disease.

GEFILLTE FISH

3 lbs mixed bream, cod, fresh haddock
3 eggs
2 carrots
1 tbsp chopped parsley
Breadcrumbs

3 onions
1 stick celery
1 oz ground almonds
Salt, pepper

Simmer the heads, skins and bones of the fish in $\frac{1}{2}$ pint water with 1 carrot sliced, the chopped celery, salt and pepper for 45 minutes. Drain. Mince and chop the rest of the fish, mix well with the parsley, ground almonds, beaten eggs and enough breadcrumbs to bind the mixture. Roll into balls. Simmer these gently in the fish stock with the other sliced carrot for 1 hour. Remove the balls from the stock, arrange a slice of carrot on top of each. Reduce the stock if necessary, and pour a little over each ball. It should set when cold. Serve cold.

Healthy Exhalations

Helena, Comtesse de Noailles, known to everyone as Madame, had two interests in life: keeping healthy and promoting the arts. These two alone would not have entitled her to a place here were it not for the strange way she combined them.

In 1865 Madame bought a lovely young Spanish girl for two bags of gold and thereafter controlled Maria Pasqua's life completely. She was entered for a Sussex convent school and Madame insisted on alterations to the curriculum, uniform and environs before Maria's arrival. Madame abhorred academic pressure on youngsters and tight clothes, so Maria studied only two of the three Rs, through a system devised by Madame, and her uniform was a Greek-style tunic and sandals. Madame also believed in fresh air and the beneficial properties of methane gas and herself kept cows near her open windows to take advantage of the 'exhalations'. On the other hand, she had the school pond drained for fear of mosquitoes.

Madame valued her own privacy, despite her somewhat dictatorial style, and although she dined in company, it was behind a two-foot high screen around her place setting. I don't know if she was served some delicacy not permitted her guests, or whether modesty dictated this action. She also travelled in a private railway carriage fitted entirely to her specification. Much of her travelling was to Calais, and she ate soft herring roe as a cure for bronchitis – so the following dish would have suited her.

HARENGS À LA CALAIS

Remove the herrings' backbones by cutting them open down the backs. Mix the roes with breadcrumbs soaked in a little milk, a small chopped onion and some parsley, pepper, salt and 2 tbsp of cream and softened butter. Place this stuffing in the cavity and press the edges together. Wrap the herrings separately and not too closely in foil and bake them in the oven. A seasoned butter goes well with this dish.

Pauper on the Continent

Largesse, sociability and eccentricity, George Mathew offered them all. He lived like a pauper on the continent for seven years to save enough money to convert his County Tipperary home into luxurious apartments for his friends and relatives. Would that we could do the same at Wes-

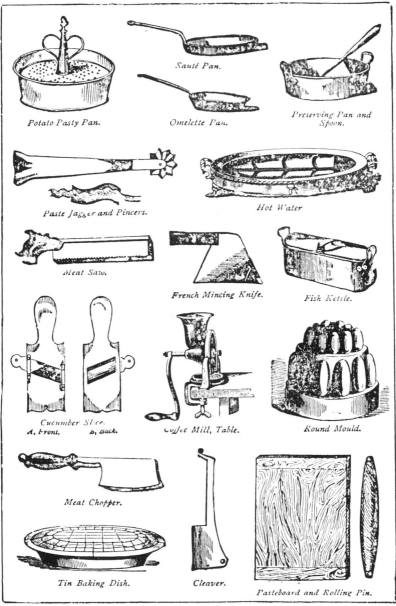

Potato Pasty Pan.

Sauté Pan.

Omelette Pan.

Preserving Pan and Spoon.

Paste Jagger and Pincers.

Hot Water

Meat Saw.

French Mincing Knife.

Fish Kettle.

Cucumber Slice.
A, Front.   B, Back.

Coffee Mill, Table.

Round Mould.

Meat Chopper.

Tin Baking Dish.

Cleaver.

Pasteboard and Rolling Pin.

Kitchen Utensils.

ton Park! Absolutely everything was laid on for Mathew's guests and even Dean Swift is reported to have succumbed to the ambiance of Thomastown Castle. What more fitting recipe for this kind-hearted eccentric than Haddock Maison, which you could of course make more lavish by using a more exotic fish.

HADDOCK MAISON

2 poached haddock steaks
1 lb potatoes
$\frac{1}{2}$ pint onion sauce
2 tbs white wine
Parsley

Oil for frying
2 large tomatoes, halved
Small dressed crab
2 tbs lemon juice, lemon wedges

Fry the peeled and diced potatoes in about an inch of oil in a frying-pan until they are golden brown. Drain them and keep warm. Gently fold the dressed crab into the onion sauce, and add the white wine and lemon juice, and plenty of chopped parsley. Adjust seasoning and reheat. Grill the tomatoes. Put the haddock steaks on a heated serving platter and pour the sauce over. Put the tomatoes and potatoes at either end, and garnish the whole with sprigs of parsley.

Navy Man God

Commander Geoffrey Spicer Simpson was appointed to lead a suicide expedition to destroy three German gunboats on Lake Tanganyika at the outbreak of the First World War. Although he survived, the journey by boat from Tilbury, by rail from Cape Town, across the Kalahari Desert into the Congo, up and over the Mitumba range and afloat downriver to Kalemir on the lake's shores seems to have unsettled his mind. He took to wearing his wife's skirt while overseeing battle preparations.

He succeeded in capturing one of the German gunboats and using it to destroy the second. While waiting for the appearance of the third the natives, who had witnessed his heroic deeds, acclaimed the Commander as 'Navy Man God' and produced little clay idols of the Admiralty's newest DSO. But Navy Man God found it difficult to adjust to success and, carried away by the praise, awe and respect, he took to having a public bath at 4.00 pm each day on the porch of his residence. Armed with a cigarette in a long holder in one hand and a glass of vermouth in the other he would appear in front of the Congolese wrapped in a big bath towel. This was removed in full view of the vast gathering who gasped to see his body covered in tattoos of flowers, birds and insects which he could move by rippling his muscles.

The third gunboat appeared one afternoon in the midst of this display. But the Commander would not attack and when the Admiralty finally recalled him on the grounds of his being unwell through 'a nervous disability' he contined to fantasize that the German gunboat would *not come out* to fight and that ever more important Navy work was about to be given to him.

Here is a genuine East African lake fish recipe cooked for Navy Man God.

NGEGE (FRIED LAKE FISH WITH GROUNDNUT SAUCE)

1 large or 2 small ngege
2 medium onions, sliced
2 tsps curry powder or spice
Salt and pepper

$\frac{1}{2}$ pint cooking oil
2 tsps groundnut paste
$\frac{1}{2}$ pint cold water

Scale and gut the fish, wash it and pat dry. Make cuts in a few places on both sides of the fish. Rub salt, pepper and curry powder in to the cuts. Heat oil in a heavy frying-pan until smoking. Put in fish, and fry without turning until brown and crisp. Turn the fish over and fry the other side in the same way. Reduce the heat, cover frying pan and cook for about 20 minutes, or until the fish is tender. Remove fish from pan carefully and place in a flat dish and keep hot. Fry the onion quickly, and scatter over the fish. Remove frying pan from heat, add groundnut paste and salt and pepper and curry powder or spice. Stir gently, adding cold water slowly. Return to the heat and simmer the sauce until it thickens.

Serves two.

Eta Beta Pi

Anyone seriously interested in the history of food, as I am, will know of Dr William Kitchiner, who lived from 1775 to 1827. His own interest in food was eccentric but none the less totally comprehensive.

Following his MD degree from Glasgow University, Kitchiner devoted his life to the study of, and writing about, food and cooking. His interest came partly from his own love of food and partly from a scientific interest in food preparation as it concerned good health. Meals at his Eta Beta Pi dining club (of which he was founder and secretary) were renowned, and invitations much sought after. These were withdrawn if not answered within twenty-four hours, and any guest who arrived late was simply not admitted. Dr Kitchiner's maxim, 'Better never than late' was strictly applied for he felt that 'the least delay' in partaking of the culinary delights 'would render them no longer worthy of men of taste'. Modern latecomers please note!

His varied and 'scientific' researches led him to numerous odd inventions, especially to do with food, and he published books with marvellous titles such as *The Pleasure of Making a Will*, *A Companion to the Telescope* and *The Housekeeper's Ledger; a plan of keeping accounts of the expenses of housekeeping. To which is added Tom Thrift's Essay on the Pleasure of Early Rising.* But such fame as Dr Kitchiner achieved stems from his work *'Apicius Redivivus or The Cook's Oracle, being six hundred receipts, the result of actual experiments instituted in the kitchen of a physician, comprising a culinary code for the rational epicure'.* (The original Apicius is in the *Poultry and Game* section.) The book is somewhat disorganized, as might be expected from such an eccentric personality but at the same time is amusing and interesting and his work has proved valuable source material for many cookery writers since.

Here is a recipe for Potted Lobster from *'Apicius Redivivus . . .'*, published in 1817. I chose this recipe particularly because I myself do many potted fish dishes at Weston Park.

POTTED LOBSTER

This must be made with fine hen lobsters, when full of spawn, boil them thoroughly, when cold, pick out all the solid meat, and pound it in a mortar – it is usual to add, by degrees (a very little) finely pounded mace, black or cayenne pepper, salt and while pounding, a little butter. When the whole is well mixed, and beat the consistence of paste, press it down hard in a preserving pot, pour clarified butter over it, and cover it with a wetted bladder.

APICIUS REDIVIVUS;

OR,

THE COOK'S ORACLE:

Wherein especially

THE ART OF COMPOSING SOUPS, SAUCES, AND FLAVOURING ESSENCES
IS MADE SO CLEAR AND EASY, BY THE QUANTITY OF EACH
ARTICLE BEING ACCURATELY STATED BY WEIGHT AND
MEASURE, THAT EVERY ONE MAY SOON LEARN
TO DRESS A DINNER, AS WELL AS THE
MOST EXPERIENCED COOK;

Being Six Hundred Receipts,

THE

RESULT OF ACTUAL EXPERIMENTS

INSTITUTED IN

THE KITCHEN OF A PHYSICIAN,

FOR THE PURPOSE OF COMPOSING

A CULINARY CODE FOR THE RATIONAL EPICURE,

AND AUGMENTING

The Alimentary Enjoyments of Private Families;

COMBINING ECONOMY WITH ELEGANCE;

AND SAVING EXPENSE TO HOUSEKEEPERS,
AND TROUBLE TO SERVANTS.

"I have taken as much pains in describing, in the fullest manner, how to make, in
the cheapest, most agreeable, and most economical way, those Dishes which daily c n-
tribute to the comforts of the middle rank of Society, as I have in directing the
composition of those *piquante* and elaborate relishes, the most ingenious and acco m-
plished "Officers of the Mouth" have invented for the entertainment of *friands*
and *voluptés*. These are so composed, as to be as agreeable and useful to the stomach,
as they are inviting to the appetite; nourishing without being inflammatory, and
satisfying without being surfeiting."—*Vide Preface, page 3.*

LONDON:

PRINTED FOR SAMUEL BAGSTER,

No. 15, PATERNOSTER-ROW,

By J. Moyes, Greville Street.

1817.

Sir Ranulph Twisleton-Wykeham-Fiennes

Sir Ranulph, not surprisingly, prefers to be known as Ranulph Fiennes and is adamant that despite what people think he does not consider himself to be an eccentric. He came up with this simple but delicious recipe which he calls Transglobe Fish Cakes. The title commemorates the fact that Ranulph circumnavigated the world by the polar route between 1979 and 1982, for which he received the Livingstone Gold Medal from the Royal Scottish Geographical Society and the Explorers' Club of New York Medal. He is an intrepid and indefatigable explorer and no doubt I shall be able to add further recipes of his to my collection following his next expedition.

TRANSGLOBE FISH CAKES

Preparation time: 15 minutes; cooking time: 20 minutes

1 large tin salmon
2 eggs
Ground black pepper

6 medium potatoes
2 tsps mixed herbs
Egg and breadcrumbs

Peel and boil (or steam) potatoes until soft. Boil eggs for five minutes. Turn salmon into large mixing bowl and add potatoes, eggs and all other ingredients. Mash up well. Make good size balls. Roll in egg and breadcrumbs. Fry until brown.

Serves 4 to 6

Wally Herbert

Another eccentric British explorer is Wally Herbert, who specializes in expeditions to the Poles, with a polar career which now spans twenty-nine years, thirteen of which have been spent in the Arctic and the Antarctic. During that time he has travelled over 20,000 miles with his dog teams. One of his many journeys was called by Lord Wilson 'a feat of endurance and courage which ranks with any in polar history'. One of Wally's most endearing features is the way in which at intervals on his journeys, and whenever there is a problem to solve, he stops for what he calls a 'brew-up' – thus remaining a tea-drinking Englishman even in the Arctic wastes.

Wally's favourite Arctic recipe, which he describes as tasty, filling and nourishing, is given here.

WALLY HERBERT'S FAVOURITE ARCTIC RECIPE

Take a chunk of walrus, seal or polar bear; examine it most carefully for any signs of trichinae; boil in salted water for half an hour and eat with one's legs apart and head thrust forward so that the drips do not soil one's polar bear pants but hit the snow safely midway between one's sealskin boots. No fork is needed – only a hunting knife. The meat in the pot is stabbed with the point of the knife, raised to the mouth and closed on with one's teeth. The left hand then takes hold of the chunk of meat, and with the right hand clasping the hunting knife, a mouth-sized piece is cut free from the main chunk by passing the knife in front of one's face (left to right) through the meat a few millimetres from the tip of one's nose. The hands are cleaned after the meal in the snow which is rubbed all over them until it melts, and the hands dried on the sides of one's sealskin boots.

WHITE MOUNTAIN FREEZER.

USED BY MRS. LINCOLN.

Endorsed and recommended by the Boston Cooking School, and used there in preference to all other freezers.

Dangerous Delicacies

Anyone interested in eccentric recipes is fascinated to find how much of our food is essentially dangerous. In this country we are unperturbed by the fact that many of the fungi we think of as mushrooms may well be lethal. In Jamaica no one gives a second thought to the fact that ackees (a fleshy vegetable) are deadly if you eat them while they're unripe. And the Japanese persist in eating their Fugu fish, even though it is known to be a killer.

FUGU

Now read carefully! There are 20 species of Fugu; one (the Safa-Fugu) is edible, the others are all poisonous. The edible species is edible only in winter, the season being October–March, and even then only certain parts of the fish are edible. The poison in the Fugu is tetrodotoxin ($C_{11}H_{17}O_8N_3$) and this is found in the ovaries, liver, entrails or sometimes in the skin itself of the fish. The skin of both sexes of Fugu has been described as 'touch and go' . . . You touch and you go?

Before cooking, the poison must be removed by a qualified cook. Government examinations are held by the official agency in each prefecture annually. Usually 1,500 cook apprentices take the examination, but only 20 per cent are successful in passing the examination to become qualified cooks.

It is reported that hundreds of people die in Japan each year from eating the wrong Fugu. Perhaps as so many die even the qualified cooks are making mistakes!

After that, the ackee seems tame in comparison. The following is a popular Jamaican dish, easily adapted.

SALT FISH AND ACKEE

1 lb salt cod	1 doz ackees (or 18 oz tin, or 4 scrambled eggs)
large onion	
$\frac{1}{4}$ lb bacon	3–4 tbs cooking oil
1 tsp pepper	small sweet red pepper cut into rings

Soak fish and bring to the boil in cold water. Prepare ackees and add to boiling cod fish. (If using tinned ackees, warm them through before arranging them with the fish; the same applies to the scrambled eggs.) When the fish is cooked, drain it, wash it and then flake it and put to keep warm. Fry bacon strips, drain and keep hot. Sauté onions and pepper in bacon fat, reserve some pepper rings for garnish. Heat oil in same pan, add fish and heat through. Arrange the fish and ackees/scrambled eggs on a hot serving dish. Garnish with bacon, onions and pepper rings.

Serves four.

Another Jamaican favourite is the one devised as a snack meal to eat while travelling, hence the name.

STAMP AND GO

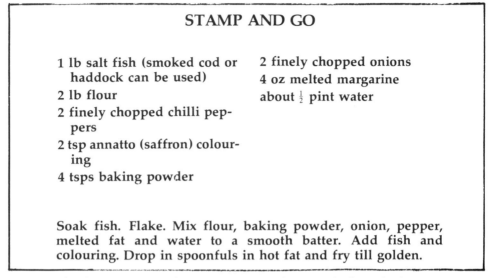

1 lb salt fish (smoked cod or haddock can be used)

2 lb flour

2 finely chopped chilli peppers

2 tsp annatto (saffron) colouring

4 tsps baking powder

2 finely chopped onions

4 oz melted margarine

about ½ pint water

Soak fish. Flake. Mix flour, baking powder, onion, pepper, melted fat and water to a smooth batter. Add fish and colouring. Drop in spoonfuls in hot fat and fry till golden.

The last recipe in this Jamaican trio has a title for which I can find no explanation. I include it because I can't resist the name, which describes the way I feel sometimes.

RUN DOWN

¾ lb shad, mackerel, saltfish or crayfish

3½ cups coconut milk

1 large onion

1 clove garlic

Sprig of thyme

2 green/sweet red peppers

2 medium tomatoes

Black pepper and vinegar to taste

1 spring onion

Soak salted fish, wash with limes, and remove bones. Boil coconut milk until oil is almost formed. Add seasoning and cook for 10 minutes. Add fish and cook until tender. Serve hot with boiled green bananas or roast breadfruit, or use as a stuffing for breadfruit.

Serves four.

POULTRY
AND
GAME

Magnus Pyke, OBE

Dr Pyke is one of those men I particularly admire who, after retiring from one job, make a major success in a totally new career – in Dr Pyke's case as a television pundit. His expertise is in the field of nutrition, but he added to my collection a recipe given to him by his friend Henry Sarson over fifty years ago – the method is that used for the startling effects still remembered in the nursery rhyme 'Sing A Song of Sixpence'. Neither Dr Pyke nor I have tried baking two dozen blackbirds, however.

TO MAKE PIES THAT BIRDS MAY BE ALIVE IN THEM, AND FLIE OUT WHEN IT IS CUT UP

Take the coffin of a great pie or patty in the bottome whereof make a hole as big as your fist, or bigger if you will, let the sides of the coffin bee somewhat higher than ordinary pies, which done, put it full of flower and bake it, and being baked, open the hole in the bottome and take out the flower. Then having a pie of the highness of the hole in the bottome of the coffin aforesaid, you then put it into the coffin, withall put into the said coffin round about the aforsaid pie as many small live birds as the empty coffin will hold besides the pie aforsaid. And this is to be done at such time as you fech the pie to the table and set before the guests: where on cutting up the lid of the great pie the birds will flie out which is to delight and pleasure those in the company. And because they shall not be altogether mocked, you shall cut open the small pie and in this sort you may make others, the like you may do with a tart.

King Three Times Over

I think that all successful soldiers and rulers have an element in their make-up which it is perhaps kindest to call eccentric. Few men have been as successful in their aims as William the Conqueror, our first Norman King.

Norman cooking and feasting revolutionized British fare, with William appreciating the political and other advantages of keeping his army and court well supplied with food and drink. He is supposed to have been thrice crowned so that he could have three coronation feasts, and introduced three major feast days, at Easter, Whitsun and Christmas, all held in different castles. Most of the feasts would have consisted of animals killed in the King's own forests. I believe it was William the Conqueror who introduced rabbits to Britain. Chicken was a luxury, so it is more than likely that on one of his feast days he indulged in the following recipe.

BLANK MANNG OF CHYKEN

1 boiling chicken, about
  1.35 kg (3 lb)
1 bouquet garni
225 g (8 oz) short grain rice
12 g ($\frac{1}{2}$ oz) caster sugar
50 g (2 oz) blanched whole
  almonds
salt
For the almond milk:
1 litre (2 pints) water
1 tsp caster sugar
50 g (2 oz) butter
1 onion, skinned
seasoning
50 g (2 oz) sugar
50 g (2 oz) ground almonds
lard or oil for frying
fresh parsley
225 g (8 oz) ground or
  pounded almonds

Make the almond milk by simmering the almonds gently in the water and sugar until all the flavour is extracted (about $1\frac{1}{2}$ hours). Strain. Place the chicken in a large saucepan, cover with boiling water, add the onion, bouquet garni and seasoning. Cover, bring to the boil and simmer until the bird is tender (about $1\frac{1}{2}$–2 hours, according to age and size). When cooked, remove from the stock, discard the skin and bones, cut the flesh into bite-sized pieces and keep warm. Cook the rice in the almond milk, adding some of the chicken stock to make up the required amount of liquid. Drain the rice but do not dry it – it should be moist. Return the rice to the saucepan and add the diced chicken, butter, sugar and ground almonds. Season well. Fry the whole almonds lightly in the oil or fat until golden. Sprinkle with a little salt. Serve the rice on a heated dish, decorated with the fried almonds and parsley.

Serves four.

Mysteries of the Orient

Chinese cooking is undoubtedly one of the world's greatest cuisines, but some of its combinations of ingredients strike me as . . . well, bizarre. Perhaps a nation with so many mouths to feed is determined to waste nothing – not even parts of birds it doesn't occur to us *can* be cooked. Did you know that Britain actually has a thriving export trade to Hong Kong in ducks' feet?

The next two recipes are again from Lawrence Leung's Zen restaurant.

DUCK TONGUES AND BROAD BEANS

100 duck tongues	400 g broad beans
1 spring onion, sliced	1 tablespoon sugar
2 slices ginger	2 teaspoons wine
salt and pepper	1 teaspoon cornstarch solution
2 cups clear soup	2 tablespoons chicken fat

1 Wash the duck tongues clean and scald them in boiling water, take them out, remove cartilages, cut the roots off and use only the tongues themselves. 2 Mix the spring onion, ginger, and salt and pepper well in a bowl, add clear soup, put in the duck tongues to cause the sauce to flood the tongues then steam tongues in the steamer for 40 minutes. 3 Having bought

---

fresh tender broad beans, skin them. Boil them in boiling soup until just tender. 4   Place soup in the pot, put the duck tongues in to boil for 5 minutes, and the beans to boil together, season them with $\frac{1}{2}$ teaspoon salt, teaspoon pepper, the sugar and wine, stir cornstarch solution in and pour boiled chicken fat over for serving.

GOLDFISH WITH DUCK WEBS

12 duck webs
(a) 1$\frac{1}{2}$ cups clear soup
     2 teaspoons Shaohsing wine
     1 teaspoon salt
     1 tablespoon chicken fat
(b) $\frac{1}{2}$ teaspoon salt
     1 teaspoon wine
     dash of pepper

lard
240 g fish colloid

2 pieces ham
adequate amount of yolk cake
1 tablespoon green peas
1 black mushroom
4 cherries
1 cup wax gourd balls
cooking oil
1 tablespoon cornstarch solution
$\frac{1}{2}$ cup cooked fresh straw mushroom pudding (halved)

1   Boil the duck webs in hot water for 10 minutes and remove their yellow skins and phalanges at the second joints; then put them in a bowl with the (a) ingredients, stir well, steam them for 30 minutes until sufficiently tender and take them out. 2   Apply lard evenly on to clean spoons, fill fish colloid in the centre of each spoon, put a ham slice on the handle, put a duck web wiped dry on it, bind them firmly with cornstarch paste to make the tail of a goldfish. Use fish colloid as the body and head of each fish, yolk cake as the back, green peas as the eyes, a piece of cherry as the mouth and of black mushroom as the gill, shape all the ingredients into the shape of goldfish; take them out, lay them on the rim of a plate and garnish them with fresh straw mushroom pudding in each space. 3   Scald wax gourd balls in oil, season them, cook them for 20 minutes and place them on the plate with the 'goldfish'. Mix the (b) ingredients well, stir the cornstarch solution in and pour the mixture over the wax gourd balls and duck webs.

The next recipe finds its way here because of its title, and because of the airy way it advises 'bone the chicken'. If you want to try this, I do recommend looking up how to bone a chicken!

DUMPOKE

Ingredients. 1 chicken, forcemeat made from rice and fresh herbs with seasoning. Mode. Bone the chicken and stuff it as nearly into shape as possible with the forcemeat, and either roast or boil it. It may be served either hot or cold, and is cut through in slices.

FIG. 26. Mutton Duck.

A Cruel Cross

The aristocracy are burdened with some cruel crosses in their names and I sympathize with a boy called Clotworthy Skeffington – fortunately he became the 2nd Earl of Masserene at the early age of fifteen. But I have to admit that I would not have joined him in a Paris prison for eighteen years rather than pay a business debt. Of course on £4,000 a year in 1770 even in prison Lord Masserene lived like a king, marrying the prison governor's daughter and having the most sumptuous meals served in the privacy of his cell. This recipe for *Canard aux olives*, preferably followed by a lavish French flan (the recipe is given in the *Puddings* section) is typical of what Masserene may have eaten.

CANARD AUX OLIVES

Ingredients: 1 large duck, $\frac{1}{4}$ lb of French olives, 2 oz of butter, some parsley, fine onions, flour and salt, $\frac{1}{4}$ pint of stock, 1 glass of light French white wine (Sauterne, Chablis, &c), 1 blade of pounded mace, 2 or 3 cloves, 4 or 5 whole peppers, and a few small pieces of bacon. Mode: Blanch the olives, cut them off the stones in spirals, and simmer them till done in a little stock and white wine. Brown some onions in butter with a pinch of flour and salt, place the duck in this with its dripping, after roasting for not more than 20 minutes. Put over a slow fire, adding the bacon, parsley and spice and a little stock, turn the duck over in this gravy and baste. When nearly done, add a bit of sugar and the olives prepared as above. Serve up the duck with the olive sauce round it.

Time: 40 minutes

Sufficient for 5 persons.

A Noted Gourmet

The *Art of Cooking*, more commonly called *The Roman Cookery Book*, is essential reading for anyone interested in the history of cooking. Apicius was probably the original author of the much altered and added-to version that we know today, which includes humble recipes alongside some truly exotic ones.

M. Gavius Apicius lived in the first century, and was a noted gourmet. Indeed, Seneca reported that Apicius committed suicide when he realized that he had spent his fortune, and could no longer live in the manner to which he had accustomed himself.

I'm not entirely sure whether flamingo is game, but since I don't know of anyone who farms them I presume their wild status entitles them to be called game.

FLAMINGO

IN PHOENICOPTERO. phoenicopterum eliberas, lavas, ornas, includis in caccabum, adicies aquam, salem, anethum et aceti modicum. Dimidia coctura alligas fasciculum porri et coriandri, et coquator. prope cocturam defritum mittis, coloras. adicies in mortarium piper, cuminum, coriandrum, laseris radicem, mentam, rutam, fricabis, suffundis acetum, adicies caryotam, ius de suo sibi perfundis. reexinanies in eundem caccabum, amulo obligas, ius perfundis et inferes. idem facies et in psittaco.

FLAMINGO. Pluck the flamingo, wash, truss, and put it in a saucepan; add water, dill, and a little vinegar. Half-way through the cooking make a bouquet of leek and coriander and let it cook [with the bird]. When it is nearly done add *defrutum* to give it colour. Put in a mortar pepper, caraway, coriander, asafœtida root, mint, rue; pound; moisten with vinegar, add Jericho dates, pour over some of the cooking-liquor. Put it in the same saucepan, thicken with cornflour, pour the sauce over the bird, and serve.

The same recipe can also be used for parrot.

ALITER: assas avem, teres piper, ligusticum, apii semen, sesamum frictum, petroselinum, mentam, cepamsiccam, caryotam; melle, vino, liquamine, aceto, oleo et defrito temperabis.

ANOTHER METHOD. Roast the bird. Pound pepper, lovage, celery-seed, grilled sesame, parsley, mint, dried onion, Jericho date. Blend with honey, wine, *liquamen*, vinegar, oil, and *defrutum**.

*For a description of *liquamen*, see p. 26; *defrutum* was must or wine reduced to a half or more by boiling.

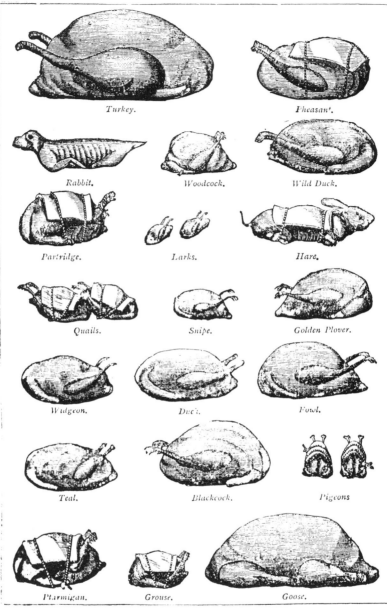

Turkey.

Pheasant.

Rabbit.

Woodcock.

Wild Duck.

Partridge.

Larks.

Hare.

Quails.

Snipe.

Golden Plover.

Widgeon.

Duck.

Fowl.

Teal.

Blackcock.

Pigeons

Ptarmigan.

Grouse.

Goose.

Poultry and Game.

Shropshire's Robin Hood

This is the man who first started me collecting eccentric recipes. He was popularly known as the Robin Hood of Shropshire and was idolized by the poor because he freely distributed among them goods and money he levied from the rich. Kynaston is an ancestor on my mother's side, the son of Sir Roger Kynaston, born in the middle of the fifteenth century. An imprudent and what would today be called 'fun-loving' life created enormous debts so that by 1482 he was forced to fly from Middle Castle, which was anyway on the point of falling into ruin through neglect. He took shelter in a cave on Nesscliffe Hill, in a wood that I still own.

From this cave Humphrey could watch travellers on the old Roman Road and observe business being carried on at the 'Ye Olde Three Pigeons' Inn which he often frequented. The then maltster of the inn was renowned for brewing his own ales and cider which he sold according to alcoholic strength at between one and two pence a gallon. The still he used is visible in the cellar today. Apart from the beer and cider, elderberry wines, spiced punches and mead were also brewed, and a recipe for mead is given in the *Drinks* section.

Kynaston's career in the area was brief but his exploits and vagaries filled the countryside around with enthusiastic reports of his courage and generosity, and he was looked after carefully by the local people. His chair remains today, cut into the sandstone of the inglenook fireplace where he rested from his adventures and enjoyed the meals prepared for him by the landlady of that time.

The local people were equally generous in looking after Kynaston's horse which grazed in the fields below his cave but which would immediately respond to his whistle by climbing the thirty-nine steps, and would kneel at his bidding. When occasion demanded, the horse was stabled in the smaller of the two rooms of the cave. The steps and rooms exist today and can easily be reached by the path – immediately opposite the Old Three Pigeons.

LIFE OF LUXURY

Kynaston was sure to have enjoyed Typsy Pork available from the inn. A young pig would be brought from market and kept in a life of luxury on a bed of clean straw and fed on boiled vegetables, potatoes, cakes and cheeses, all washed down with the ale slops from the large vats. The pig spent more of its time sleeping as a result of the alcohol consumed and consequently grew at an alarming rate. At the right time the animal was slaughtered, cut up and placed in salt-petre brine. The pork would then be roasted in the baker's oven, or boiled in cider, and served with the meat juices which would be boiled and thickened with honey and breadcrumbs.

This traditional dish was supplied by the inn's own pigs until recently when it had to cease, to comply with the stringent hygienic conditions imposed by the EEC. Humphrey Kynaston is remembered to this day by the local people, the cave at Nesscliffe is visited by many people and it is reported that he still visits the Pigeons Inn and has been seen on many occasions. If this is so, his visits are friendly and as welcome as they used to be so many years ago.

In all its time the inn has supplied many a weary traveller with a well-earned rest and good food and drink and until the turn of the century it also took care of the many horses which also needed refreshment. The stables have been converted into the restaurant and a false ceiling put into this room hides the original hay loft.

Here is a recipe from the Pigeons Inn which I urge you to try.

SPICED GAME POTTAGE

2 old well hung cock pheasants, roasted and cut up fine without the bones.

$2\frac{3}{4}$ pints game stock

1 oz barley

1 tsp mixed spice

1 calf's foot

1 rabbit's foot

2 lbs dried carrots, turnips, onions, and celery

1 bunch of herbs i.e. sage, rosemary, tarragon, parsley.

Method **Prepare a broth from the above ingredients, except the rabbit's foot. Remove and dice the calf's foot when cooked and eat with mauchet bread (granary loaf). This dish was always left on top of the fire and would be topped up during the day as needed.**

The rabbit's foot was for luck.

Between 3,500 and 4,000 pies are sold each week at Porters in Covent Garden, suggesting that the British really are the biggest pie eaters of all time. Here are two recipes, one vegetarian, for pies which are served at my restaurant.

PORTERS LAMB AND APRICOT PIE

1 lb diced lamb (best cut leg)
4 oz onion
2 oz flour
pinch of mixed herbs
water

15 oz tin apricot halves
4 oz butter
2 tsp mint sauce
1 oz tomato purée
puff pastry

Fry the lamb and the finely chopped onions in a large pot until the lamb is browned. For this use only half of the butter. Add the tomato puree to this, also the mixed herbs and mint sauce. After simmering for 3 minutes add water to cover all ingredients and bring to the boil, reduce heat and simmer for 30 minutes. When meat is tender take it from the stock. Make a roux from the butter and flour and thicken the stock, add a little of the juice from the apricots, season and allow to simmer for 5 minutes. Add sauce to meat and apricots and place in a pie dish. Cover and bake with puff pastry top.

The old baker's oven at the Olde Three Pigeons, although long since gone, has left its tell-tale outline on the rear wall, and it would be on this that many of the breads and pies would be prepared and baked. Favourites of that time were Pigeon and Redcurrant Pie and Fowey Pie (in the *Puddings* section). These were usually eaten off a bread trencher to sup up the juices.

PIGEON AND REDUCURRANT PIE

Bone and dice very young pigeons and seal in chicken fat. Fry some chopped onions in the chicken fat and some bacon pieces, a clove of garlic and a port wine. Place all this into a deep pie dish; put the first season's redcurrants on the top and fill up with a pigeon stock. Cover with a tightly sealed hot water paste and bake slowly in the bottom of a baker's oven. This used to be done after the bread had been made and the ovens were turned off. Eat with baked rice and elderberry wine.

VARIOUS KINDS OF POULTRY, WHEN IN SEASON, PRICE.

Poultry.	When in Season.	When Best.	Average Price.
Chickens	February to October...	July to September......	2/0 to 3/0 each.
Ducklings	February to August...	May to July	2/6 to 3/6 each.
Ducks	August to February ..	September and October	3/0 to 4/0 each.
Fowls	All the Year	June to October.........	2/6 to 3/6 each.
Geese	September to February	October and November	0/7 to 0/10 per lb.
Green Geese	May to August	June	6/0 to 10/0 each.
Guinea Fowl	February to August...	Summer	3/0 to 4/0 each.
Larks	October to December...	November	2/0 to 3/0 per doz.
Pigeons	August to April.........	Winter	0/9 to 1/0 each.
Pigeons (Bordeaux)	All the Year	Winter.....................	1/0 to 1/4 each.
Rabbits	All the Year	October to February...	0/6 to 0/8 per lb.
Rabbits (Ostend) ...	All the Year .	October to February .	0/7 to 0/8 per lb.
Turkeys	October to March	November to January	0/9 to 1/0 per lb.
Wheatears	September to March...	September and October	1/0 each.

VARIOUS KINDS OF GAME, WHEN IN SEASON, PRICE.

Game.	When in Season.	When Best.	Average Price.
Blackcock	August to November...	September and October	2/6 to 3/6 per brace.
Capercailzie	September to April ...	January to March ...	
Ducks (Wild)	October to September..	November & December	2/0 to 3/0 per brace.
Grouse	August to November...	September	3/6 to 5/0 per brace.
Hares	September to March...	October and November	3/6 to 6/0 each.
Leverets	August and September	August.....................	3/0 to 4/0 each.
Partridges	September to February	October and November	4/0 to 5/0 per brace.
Pheasants	October to February...	Winter.....................	5/0 to 6/0 per brace.
Plovers	October to February...	Winter.....................	1/0 to 1/6 each.
Ptarmigan	September to April ...	September	1/6 to 2/0 each.
Quail	September to February	September and October	1/0 to 1/6 each.
Snipe	October to February...	October and November	2/6 to 3/6 per brace.
Teal	October to February ..	October and November	1/0 to 1/6 each.
Venison	September to January	September and October	1/0 to 2/0 per lb.
Widgeon	October to February...	October and November	1/0 to 1/6 each.
Woodcock	October to February...	October and November	3/6 to 5/6 per brace.

Mayonnaise of Salmon

Raised Pie.

Lobster Salad.

Cherry Tartlets.

Game Pie.

Fancy Pastry.

Open Tart.

Tomato and Cucumber Salad.

Ratafia Pudding.

Pigeon Pie.

Meat Pie.

Supper Dishes.

PORTERS PIE

2 oz sliced green beans
2 oz peeled and diced carrots
2 oz leek cut in $\frac{1}{2}$ inch rings
1 clove of garlic
2 oz corn niblets
2 oz red kidney beans (soaked overnight)
1 oz tomato puree
salt and pepper to taste

2 oz peeled and diced potatoes
2 oz finely cut white cabbage
2 oz courgettes (cut in $\frac{1}{4}$ in rings)
2 oz fine fleurets of cauliflower
2 oz chick peas (soaked overnight)
1 oz mild curry powder
1 oz cornflour
2 oz butter

shortcrust pastry made with wholemeal flour

Cook the kidney beans and chick peas in boiling water until tender, cool and then wash them and allow to drain. Cook the green beans, carrots, cabbage, leeks, cauliflower, corn and potatoes together in boiling salted water until tender. Save the water. Crush the garlic and fry in the butter; add to this the courgettes and gently cook, to this add the tomato purée and curry powder. Add the water the vegetables were cooked in to the courgettes, bring to the boil and thicken with the cornflour, simmer for 5 minutes. Add the seasoning to the sauce and then put all the vegetables to the sauce. Place the mixture into a deep pie dish and cover with a wholemeal pie lid, bake.

Disraeli, a Countess and a Parrot

I have a particular interest in parrots, as part of the folklore of Weston Park is the parrot given by Benjamin Disraeli to Selina, third Countess of Bradford. Disraeli was obsessed with her although she was quite happily married to my great-great-grandfather. He even proposed to her sister in order to get closer to her. But the proposal was sensibly turned down.

Disraeli and the Countess conducted a long correspondence – of friendship on her part but of something more on his. We still have 1.100 letters which he wrote to her and although he was motivated by affection this was not the only topic on which he wrote and the letters make highly amusing reading. They contain for example Disraeli's definition of a lawyer: 'To get on, to get honour, to get honest.' Then, in other letters, Disraeli makes references to food: 'I don't at all mind a bad dinner because I make it a rule never to eat it . . .' He described 'a most incongruous dinner at the German Embassy' which took place in 1876:

'I sate between Lady Derby and Constance who hate each other and who both, in their time, had confidentially imparted this reciprocity of amiable sentiment to me. The dinner was something unearthly – impossible to conceive where so many dark, hard dishes could have been collected and what cooks of Pandemonium could have prepared them. I literally touched nothing, which was noticed by our host – but I afterwards heard from Dear Ida that she had fared like myself and had elicited from Lord Munster the same remark. She called my attention to the most wondrous dish of salmon, which would have been condemned at Billingsgate as unfit for human food!'

To revert to the parrot. It was supposedly male and sat in its cage in the Orangery at Weston for twenty-five years until one day – it laid an egg! For the next twenty-three days an egg was found at the bottom of the cage and on the twenty-fourth day the parrot itself was found at the bottom of the cage – dead! However they had it stuffed and it can still be seen today.

Trust Mrs Beeton to come up trumps with something really outrageous for this section. I have a sneaking suspicion that you would find some opposition, either from the Public Health Authority or the RSPCA, if you embarked on this recipe for Parrot Pie but nevertheless I include it for its novelty value.

PARROT PIE

Ingredients:1 dozen paraqueets, a few slices of beef (under-done cold beef is best for this purpose), 4 rashers of bacon, 3 hard-boiled eggs, minced parsley and lemon-peel, pepper and salt, stock, puff-paste. Mode: Line a pie-dish with the beef cut into slices, over them place 6 of the paraqueets, dredge with flour, fill up the spaces with the egg cut in slices and scatter over the seasoning. Next put the bacon, cut in small strips, then paraqueets and fill up with the beef, seasoning all well. Pour in stock or water to nearly fill the dish, cover with puff-paste, and bake for 1 hour.

Time: 1 hour.

Sufficient for 5 or 6 persons.

Seasonable at any time.

Another Mrs Beeton recipe that warrants inclusion for the name alone is Pooloot. Despite its title it is delicious.

POOLOOT

Ingredients: 1 fowl, 1 lb of rice, 1 quart of stock, 8 onions, 1 tablespoonful of ground ginger, a few thin rashers of bacon, 6 hard-boiled eggs, 1 lemon, butter for frying, pepper corns, cardamoms. Mode: Truss the fowl as for boiling, boil the rice for 5 minutes and drain, and put fowl and rice into a stewpan with the stock, over a slow fire. Pound 4 of the onions, and squeeze out the juice, and add with the ginger tied in a bag and the juice of the lemon. When the fowl is sufficiently done, take it out and keep hot while the rice is drying before the fire. Have ready the rest of the onions sliced and fried, cut up the fowl, and fry it in the same butter, pile the rice in the centre of a dish with the joints of fowl on the top, and over these the onions. Strew over the peppercorns and cardamoms and garnish with the eggs and fried bacon. Time: To boil the fowl, $\frac{3}{4}$ hour.

Another doyenne of early cookery books, Elizabeth Raffald, produces a recipe to vie with Mrs Beeton's in causing alarm at the Royal Society for the Protection of Birds.

TO MAKE A SPARROW DUMPLING

Mix half a pint of good milk, with three eggs, a little salt, and as much flour as will make it a thick batter, put a lump of butter rolled in pepper and salt in every sparrow, mix them in the batter, and tie them in a cloth, boil them one hour and a half, pour melted butter over them, and serve them up.

Medieval recipe books are a constant source of delight to me, for the language alone. In fact if you translate them many of the dishes are more than palatable and some of them would even be recognizable today. Since so few people had their own teeth beyond an early age a large number of the dishes are soft and pappy. On the other hand our medieval ancestors liked to get what teeth they had into a good piece of roast meat – venison in particular. One dish which was reserved for very special occasions, like coronation feasts, was peacock, roasted and served in its own feathers. I have never tried it myself but I'm told that it doesn't taste particularly good, and is rather dry and tasteless unless you baste it really well.

107

PECOKKES

At a feeste roiall pecokkes shall be dight on this manere.

Take and flee off the skynne with the fedurs (*feathers*), tayle, and the nekke, and the hed theron; then take the skyn with all the fedurs, and lay it on a table abrode; and strawe theron grounden comyn; then take the pecokke, and roste hym, and endore (*baste*) hym with rawe zolkes of egges; and when he is rosted take hym of, and let hym coole awhile, and take and sowe hym in his skyn, and gilde his combe, and so serve hym forthe with the last cours (*course*).

If your status didn't warrant peacock in feathers then you would probably have enjoyed another medieval dish, which is unusual but delicious, despite its off-putting name.

GARBAGE

Take fayre garbagys of chykonys, as þe hed, þe fete, þe lyuerys, an þe gysowrys; washe hem clene, an caste hem in a fayre potte, and caste þer to freysshe brothe of Beef or ellys of moton, an let it boyle; an a lye it wyth brede, an ley on Pepir an Safroun, Maces, Clowyse, an a lytil verious an salt, an serue forth in the maner as a Sewe.

A more up-to-date version

Giblets
1 lb chicken hearts and gizzards
$\frac{1}{2}$ pint brown stock, broth, or stock cube and water
1 tsp salt
$\frac{1}{4}$ tsp each ground black pepper, mace, saffron (optional)
pinch ground cloves
$\frac{1}{2}$ tsp ground sage

1 lb chicken livers
$\frac{1}{4}-\frac{1}{2}$ cup breadcrumbs
1 tsp cider vinegar or lemon juice
2 tbsp chopped parsley

Put the giblets in a saucepan, add the stock and bring to the boil. Simmer for half an hour. Add the chicken livers, and simmer for a further 5 minutes. Add all the seasonings except the cider vinegar/lemon juice, and the breadcrumbs. Stir until the sauce is well thickened. Add the cider vinegar/lemon juice just before serving. The sauce will be smoother if placed in a blender after the chicken livers have been added and simmered; the seasonings should be added at this stage, and the whole blended until smooth.

Barbara Cartland

Authoress and playwright, Barbara Cartland is an extremely successful woman who has carved her own niche in the world and holds her own strong opinions on every subject. Apart from her best-selling romantic novels she is well known for her pioneering work with health food and attributes her energy to a combination of honey and vitamin pills. She is a charming and generous hostess and her chef Nigel Gordon is clearly 'a treasure'. This is a recipe devised by him for Barbara Cartland's book *The Romance of Food.* I was particularly attracted to it as Miss Cartland tells me that game has always come into the category of aphrodisiacs. Apparently Hungarian women thought pheasant dishes helped to attract men when one was no longer young.

PHEASANT WITH FOIE GRAS SAUCE

1 young pheasant
50 g/2 oz butter
225 g/8 oz sliced button mushrooms

145 g/5 oz pâté de foie gras
150 ml/¼ pint single cream
150 ml/¼ pint red wine
salt and black pepper

Roast the pheasant in a hot oven, 220 °C, 425 °F, gas 7, for 40 minutes. While the pheasant is cooking, make the sauce. Melt the butter, add the mushrooms and cook gently for 5 minutes or so. Mix the pâté with the cream until smooth and add to the mushrooms along with the red wine, salt and pepper. Stir until hot and simmer for 5 minutes. Remove the pheasant from the oven and slice thinly, then pour over the sauce. Serve immediately.

Serves three.

Fig. 40. Chicken Salad.

'We'll Start Again Tomorrow'

William Beckford was a typical eighteenth-century eccentric – fabulously wealthy, but as suspicious of his peers as they were of his way of life. Left a million pounds by his father, he had done the Grand Tour before he was twenty-one, in the style only afforded by the very rich. After years of travelling, Beckford devoted his time and energy to manic developments of the family home at Fonthill in Wiltshire – rebuilding it many times. An impatient man, he wanted his every idea implemented yesterday, often with disastrous results. Still, when it stood, the Abbey (which perhaps should more properly have been called the Folly) was described by *The Times* as the most exuberant example of the Gothic Revival.

An incident about Beckford which I particularly enjoyed reading concerns the building of a tower nearly 300 feet high, which he swore would be completed by Christmas. He started with inadequate foundations, and progressed, with drunken labourers working in twenty-four hour shifts and poor building materials, to his Christmas dinner in the new premises. But the bricks were not established, the mortar not dry, and the beams swung alarmingly. As his staff carried the enormous meal from the kitchen into the dining-room, the kitchen collapsed like a card house behind them.

May you have no such disaster with this turkey recipe. If by any chance it turns out not how you expected, may you have Beckford's equanimity to say 'No matter, we'll start again tomorrow.'

A recipe for Christmas pudding is given in the *Puddings* section.

WILLIAM BECKFORD'S ROAST TURKEY CHRISTMAS DINNER

To Roast a Turkey

When you have dressed your turkey as before, truss its head down to the legs, then make your forcemeat, take the crumbs of a penny loaf, a quarter of a pound of beef suet shred fine, a little sausage meat, or veal scraped and pounded exceeding fine, nutmeg, pepper, and salt to your palate, mix it up lightly with three eggs, stuff the craw with it, spit it, and lay it down a good distance from the fire, keep it clear and brisk, singe, dust, and baste it several times with cold butter, it makes the froth stronger than basting it with the hot out of the dripping-pan, and makes the turkey rise better: when it is enough, froth it up as before, dish it up, pour on your dish the same gravy as for the boiled turkey, only put in browning instead of cream: garnish with lemon and pickles, and serve it up; if it be a middle size it will require one hour and a quarter roasting.

To Make Sauce for a Turkey

As you open your oysters, put a pint into a bason, wash them out of their liquor, and put them in another bason: when the liquor is settled, pour it clean off into a saucepan, with a little white gravy, a tea spoonful of lemon pickle, thicken it with flour and a good lump of butter, boil it three or four minutes, put in a spoonful of good thick cream, put in your oysters, keep shaking them over the fire till they are quite hot, but do not let them boil, it will make them hard and look little.

Fig. 33. Birds and Spinach on Toast.

Viscount Weymouth

I have come across Alexander Weymouth a few times over the years, mostly at social occasions in London. It is no secret that he has probably the most perfect marital arrangement of any married couple today – his wife lives in Paris and they see each other by agreement!

Viscount Weymouth lives part of the year at Longleat and the rest in France, writes, paints brilliantly and enjoys life. I am pleased to include his squirrel recipes in this collection, and particularly so when they are accompanied by his splendid introduction.

SOME SQUIRREL STARTERS

Alexander Weymouth's Guide to eating Squirrels

It is the grey squirrels, fortunately, which are good to eat, and not their unrelated red namesakes, whose habitat they have usurped. Perhaps if we can eat enough of the grey ones the delightful red squirrels of our childhood memory will eventually return to us.

But let me start with some words of warning. If the grey squirrels are taken after feasting on fir or pine shoots, their meat will taste of turpentine: in which case it is advisable to serve them accompanied by a glass of Retsina white wine. Yet such disguise is unnecessary if they are taken from hardwood forests.

There are two further problems in the preparation of squirrels for eating. The first is that they have too many small bones. And secondly, guests of a squeamish disposition, who are unaccustomed to such delicacies, may suddenly lose their appetite when confronted by the sight of a rodent on their plate.

The solution is to prepare the squirrel for consumption in such a way that its bodily form is no longer clearly discernible. You should start by removing all the meat from the carcass. This is achieved by steaming it over a court bouillion for approximately 1 hour, or until it comes away easily from the bone. Then leave the meat to cool, and make use of it later in any of the three recipes given below. Each was devised especially to suit my palate by Mary Wiltshire, my esteemed cook and housekeeper.

SQUIRREL MOULD ON NETTLES WITH SCRUMPY SAUCE

mould:
1 grey squirrel
2 carrots (sliced)
1 onion (chopped)
$\frac{1}{2}$ red pepper (chopped)
Salt and pepper to taste
1 cup Wessex scrumpy or
  rough cider
Aspic jelly mix

sauce:
1 teaspoon oil
2 teaspoons tomato purée
1 tablespoon single cream
Salt and pepper to taste
$\frac{1}{2}$ cup Wessex scrumpy or
  rough cider
Cornflour to thicken. Stewed nettles to serve.

Makes about 10 portions

Method: Use all the vegetables raw at this stage. Grease as many portions of an egg poacher as needed. Layer squirrel, sliced onion, sliced carrot, red pepper, and a couple of peppercorns, carry on until mould is full, finishing with a layer of squirrel on top. Add a little salt and pepper to taste, and a little scrumpy. Poach until veg is tender, about $\frac{1}{2}$ hr. Leave to cool. Mix aspic jelly cube with the scrumpy, pour over cool mixture and leave to set. These can be made well in advance of dinner, and left in refrigerator or even frozen until needed. Serve on a bed of stewed nettles, cover with scrumpy sauce, which is easily made by combining all the sauce ingredients together in a saucepan, bringing to the boil, and thickening to individual taste with cornflour.

SQUIRREL FAGGOTS IN SQUIRREL SOUP

1 squirrel
1 onion
Salt and pepper
Wessex scrumpy or rough
  cider
Sesame seeds
6 peppercorns
3 bay leaves
2 slices of bread soaked in
  scrumpy
2 fluid oz apple vinegar

3 tablespoons sweet red wine
1 tablespoon Worcestershire
  sauce
8 prunes (stoned)
4 oz black olives (pitted)
6 capers
1 tinned sweet pimento
Tomato purée
4 oz liver
Chicken stock

Stand squirrel meat in scrumpy for $\frac{1}{2}$ hr. Add onions, then boil until tender, adding more scrumpy if necessary. Soak bread in scrumpy then mix bayleaves, peppercorns, sesame seeds and pimento to make a paste. When the onions are tender, add the wine, black pepper, Worcestershire sauce, prunes, olives, capers, tomato purée, pimentoes and the sesame seed paste. Halve the mixture. Liquidize half the mixture, add 1 cup chicken stock, $\frac{1}{2}$ cup scrumpy and a dash of cream for the soup. To the other half of mixture, add the minced liver and form into balls and bake in a hot oven for about 30 mins. – Float the faggots in the soup when ready to serve.

SQUIRREL PASTIES WITH HALLUCINOGENIC MUSHROOMS AND SORREL CREAM

pasties:

1 grey squirrel

2 oz suet

2 hard-boiled eggs (chopped)

1 large onion

2 oz red pepper (chopped)

8 stuffed olives

2 oz raisins

4 oz edible fungi selected
    according to taste and
    expertise

A little stem of ginger

Salt and pepper

cream:

$\frac{1}{2}$ lb sorrel leaves

2 oz butter

$\frac{1}{2}$ pt Wessex or rough cider

$\frac{1}{2}$ lb chopped potatoes

$\frac{1}{2}$ pt single cream and goat's
    milk

Salt and pepper

pastry:

8 oz plain flour

2 oz suet

1 lightly beaten egg

Wessex scrumpy (or rough
    cider) to bind

PASTRY: Combine the flour, suet and beaten egg adding a little scrumpy at a time until the dough is at a rolling out consistency.

FILLING: Put a little oil into a frying pan, and fry chopped onions and mushrooms until tender, transfer to thick-bottomed saucepan; add red peppers, squirrel meat, salt and pepper, and a little goat's milk, bring to the boil stirring all the time to avoid sticking, adding more goat's milk when necessary, to bind mixture together and keep moist. Roll out the dough and cut into shapes of individual choice. In the middle of each shape, put a small heap of the squirrel mixture, add a little chopped olives, chopped hard-boiled eggs, chopped ginger and a few raisins. Fold the dough over the mixture, pressing the edges together and sealing. Brush with egg and milk mixture and bake for about 30 minutes in a moderate oven, gas mark 4, electric 350 °F 170 °C.

CREAM SAUCE: Wash and rinse sorrel. Melt butter in a saucepan and add the sorrel, stir over a moderate heat until the sorrel wilts, stir in the scrumpy and bring to the boil, add the potato with salt and simmer for about $\frac{1}{2}$ hour. Liquidize, return to the saucepan and adjust the seasoning, add the cream/goat's milk mix and warm up. Do not allow to boil. Pour it over the pasties and serve.

Makes about 12 small pasties

The last recipe of this *Poultry and Game* section comes from the original Mrs Raffald recipe book. It takes only a little imagination to realize what a decorative centre-piece this would make for a large party, although modern cooks might prefer to cook the pigeons first and take them off the bone.

A THATCHED HOUSE PYE

Take an earthen dish that is pretty deep, rub the inside with two ounces of butter, then spread over it two ounces of vermicelli, make a good puff paste, and roll it pretty thick, and lay it on the dish; take three or four pigeons, season them very well with pepper and salt, and put a good lump of butter in them, and lay them in the dish with the breast down, and put a thick lid over them, and bake it in a moderate oven; when enough, take the dish you intend for it, and turn the pye on to it, and the vermicelli will appear like a thatch, which gives it the name of thatched house pye.

BIRD BEING SINGED.

118

CONFECTIONERY
AND
CAKES

Dennis Severs

ennis Severs has restored an eighteenth-century house at Spitalfields in East London to all its former glory and lives in it as he might have done two hundred years ago without the benefit of modern trappings like gas and electricity! Several times a week he shows people around the house and gives them an intimation of what it must have been like to live in the house when it and its neighbours were inhabited by prosperous businessmen.

Spitalfields is rather like Covent Garden where I have my restaurant, in that as the traditional trade of the area has run down people have moved in with new ideas and small businesses and although there is still a long way to go Spitalfields may one day be fashionable again. If it is, it will be in no small part due to people like Dennis Severs, whose involvement with the past leads other people to regard them as eccentric, but who in my view make a lot of sense.

This is a recipe that Dennis gave me which makes full use of the leftovers from the local market.

'Being just on the edge of the colourful three-hundred-year-old Spitalfields fruit market, the gutters are teeming with abandoned fruit and vegetables which are just a little too ripe to be sold. Over some time my footman and I have developed a mixture which, when coupled with this rotting fruit, makes a delicious cake.'

DENNIS SEVERS' GUTTER GÂTEAU

$\frac{1}{2}$ lb sugar
2 eggs
$\frac{1}{4}$ tsp salt
1 tsp almond essence (optional)
approx 1 lb rotting fruit

1 lb butter
$\frac{3}{4}$ lb sifted flour
1 tsp vanilla
$\frac{1}{4}$ lb walnuts

One hour before baking build large coal fire in range, which should be at its hottest at time of baking. Send footman (undressed) into market to collect quantity of rotting bananas, peaches, mangoes, apricots, apples, kiwi fruit, or any other fruit that is festering. Bring home, wash and separate the ill from the dead. Cream the sugar and butter, and add one egg at a time. Add the ill fruit, coarsely chopped, and vanilla, keeping in mind the relationship between the dry ingredients and the amount of moisture. Mix together the dry ingredients plus walnuts, and add to mixture. Bake until your toothpick tells you it is done.

THE TWO INFALLIBLE POWERS.
THE POPE & BOVRIL.

Pamela Stephenson

Pamela Stephenson came over to Britain from Australia to prove that you don't have to be male to be a good comic. Naturally enough, this upset a lot of people who don't like to see the old traditions threatened and she came in for a lot of criticism for not toeing the line, and for being always and inimitably herself. Her success in 'Not The Nine o'clock News' and on the British stage has recently been followed up by a stint in New York on 'Saturday Night Live', the ultimate live satire show, in which she portrayed US politicians, rock stars and of course First Ladies!

PAMELA STEPHENSON'S PIOUS SURPRISE
BIRTHDAY CAKE

1. With the help of an experienced joiner, construct a large wooden cylinder about $1\frac{1}{2}$ metres in diameter and $1\frac{1}{4}$ metres high.

2. Acquire a sturdy wooden platform at least 1 centimetre thick. Add small wheels or rollers underneath and paint the upper surface and edges silver.

3. Browse in an art supply shop to find some white, light-weight paper, the kind that has a texture not unlike the effect of icing. Stretch this paper across one end of the cylinder and glue it around the circumference. Sprinkle some sugar and a bit of glitter on the top.

4. Using fancy paper and ribbon, decorate the outside of the cylinder as lavishly as possible to look like a giant cake-frill and attach large, individual candle-holders with coloured candles to the upper circumference.

5. Find out if the Pope is free to appear on the night of your party.* Don't let him wear his mitre on his head as he then won't fit inside the cylinder . . . better to have him in that flattish round skull-cap-type thingy instead.

6. If your Pope is hard of hearing, you will have to improvise a visual paging system. Simply install a small red light inside the cylinder which can be operated by a switch on the outside. Alternatively you could practise shouting "yúmpìn̄zylötté!", the Polish word for "jump!", through a loud-hailer.

7. When the guests are assembled after dinner, ask His Holiness to crouch on the platform and place the cylinder over him. There won't be much air in there, so position your trumpeters quickly and light the candles.

8. Wheel out the cake with as much ceremony as possible, preferably while Happy Birthday is being played following the appropriate ecclesiastical fanfare.

9. On second thoughts, maybe you should drill a few unobtrusive air holes on the outside of the cylinder. Another humane touch would be to fire-proof His Holiness's vestments in case they catch alight from the candles.

10. Invite the Birthday Boy or Girl to blow out the candles. On the hurrahs, cue the Pope to leap out through the paper and bless everyone, kiss the ground, and then he is free to mingle, get pickled, and run off with the punk designer in the see-through mini.

*If not, find a look-alike. There is a Welsh garage attendant called Mr Meredith who is an excellent surrogate. Hire his costume from Bermans and Nathans.

Afternoon Teas

HIMALAYAN, FORMOSA, ENGLISH BREAKFAST, and RUSSIAN TEAS.

CHOICEST IMPORTED.

CAREFULLY PUT UP IN 1-4 LB. PACKAGES, BY MAIL. PRICE LIST ON REQUEST.

TRADE MARK.

F. C. LORD, Agent,

WEST ROXBURY DISTRICT,

BOSTON, MASS., U.S.A.

Send for Circulars and Testimonials.

APPROVED BY MRS. LINCOLN.

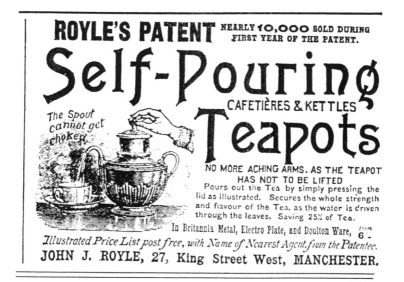
124

Another recipe from Barbados I've included just for its name!

TO MAKE BARBADOES JUMBALLS

Beat very light the yolks of four eggs and the whites of eight with a spoonful of rose water, and dust in a pound of treble refined sugar, then put in three quarters of a pound of the best fine flour, stir it lightly in, grease your tin sheets, and drop them in the shape of a macaroon, and bake them nicely.

Pickles and Tea

As a restaurateur, I despair of Mr Edward Eyre, an odd Irishman who cared little what he ate, providing it was sweets or pickles, served with tea or cold water. Despite this frugality, he spent a phenomenal amount of money during his lifetime, and was most often in debt. Perhaps it was the lavish lifestyle of his dogs, whom he dubbed his daughters and heiresses, and his own foppish dress which were his undoing.

These two early recipes for sweets suit Edward Eyre perfectly – particularly the second, which he would have enjoyed while riding around in his glass coach.

TO MAKE LEMON DROPS

Dip a lump of treble refined loaf sugar in water, boil it stiffish, take it off, rub it with the back of a silver spoon to the side of your pan, then grate in some lemon-peel, boil it up, and drop it on paper; if you want it red put in a little cochineal.

TO MAKE PEPPERMINT DROPS TO CARRY IN THE POCKET

Take one pound of treble refined sugar, beat it fine and sift it through a lawn sieve, then mix it with the whites of two eggs, beat it to a thick froth, then add sixty drops of the oil of peppermint and beat them all well together, then with a tea-spoon drop it upon fine cap paper, the size of half a nutmeg, and put them upon the hearth to dry, the next day take them off, and they are fit for use.

Maggie Black

When I decided to pull my collection of eccentric recipes into book form, one of the first people I spoke to was Maggie Black, a cookery journalist and historian who has done valuable research for me in the past on traditional British recipes for some of my restaurants. Here are two cakes from her own collection of historical recipes. The first is a Shropshire Groaning Cake. This is particularly interesting to me as Shropshire is my own county and I am keen to see local recipes perpetuated or revived. A Groaning Cake was served at a christening or after a birth, which presumably explains the strange name.

A BLESSING AND A GIFT

In some areas, the pieces of cake were cut from the middle so that by the time the child was christened, there was a central hole large enough to pass the baby through. The first person who met the christening procession on the way to church was given a piece of cake and expected to give a blessing and a gift (cash!) in return. The same idea lay behind giving cake to visitors. It varied in size with the number of well-wishers expected

but was always large, as a suitably optimistic omen for the child's future.

The original recipe for this cake used $2\frac{1}{2}$ lb flour, $\frac{1}{2}$ lb each butter and lard, 4 lb currants, $\frac{1}{2}$ lb candied peel, $\frac{3}{4}$ lb chopped almonds, salts of ammonia, eggs, sugar and spices. It was 18 inches across. This is a practical, smaller version raised with bicarbonate of soda and cream of tartar.

SHROPSHIRE GROANING CAKE

1 lb plain flour
1 tsp bicarbonate of soda
2 oz lard
1 tsp ground cinnamon
$\frac{1}{2}$ tsp grated nutmeg
$\frac{1}{2}$ lb sultanas
$\frac{1}{4}$ lb finely chopped citron
   peel
1 oz each grated orange and
   lemon rind
2 or 3 eggs, depending on size
2 tbsp rum

2 tsp cream of tartar
4 oz butter
$\frac{1}{2}$ lb light soft brown sugar
$\frac{1}{2}$ tsp ground allspice
$1-1\frac{1}{2}$ lb currants
$\frac{1}{4}$ lb blanched almonds,
   ground with a little
   rose-water

Mix the flour and leavening in a large bowl. Rub in the fats. Mix together the sugar and spices, and add to the flour. Mix in the fruit and almonds, using sultanas or the extra $\frac{1}{2}$ lb currants as you wish. Mix in the peel and rind. Beat the eggs and rum, and use the mixture to make a stiff dough. Grease and flour a large baking sheet. Shape the dough on the sheet into a round about 9 inches across and $2\frac{1}{2}-3$ inches high in the centre. It should be slightly domed. Neaten and push up the edge into a shallow rim. Bake for $1\frac{1}{2}-2$ hours at 325° F/160° C/Gas 3. The cake should be resilient and brown.

Make sure the baking sheet is large enough. The cake will spread.

THE BRITISH BAKER, AUGUST 12, 1949 *Phone:* Temple Bar 5273. *Telegrams:* Buns. Phone. London

The BRITISH BAKER

BAKING CONFECTIONERY. FLOUR & PURVEYING TRADES

THE LEADING ORGAN OF THE

Circulating throughout the World among Bread & Biscuit Bakers Pastry-cooks Cake Manufacturers & Refreshment Purveyors

Vol. CXIX. No. 7 [Registered as a Newspaper] AUGUST 12, 1949 PUBLISHED WEEKLY **3d.** Annual Subscription **20/-**

Another cake recipe from Maggie Black. It includes of all things, sauerkraut. This cake was evolved by exiled Protestants, driven from South Germany to America from Luther's time onward. Their religion, farming past, and poverty all forbade them to waste a morsel of food. So when they wanted to make their traditional applesauce cakes and lacked fruit, they turned to a preserve which they always had at hand, and flavoured it with the Caribbean beans which their Dutch neighbours used. By the nineteenth century, they had developed a cake very like this one.

MENNONITE SPICY CHOCOLATE CAKE

5 oz unsalted butter
4 small eggs
9 oz all-purpose flour
1 tsp baking powder
$\frac{1}{2}$ tsp salt

10 oz white sugar
8 fl oz water
2 oz cocoa powder
1 tsp baking soda
4 oz drained sauerkraut

Cream the butter and sugar, whisking until fluffy. Beat in the eggs one at a time with a sprinkling of flour. Mix and sift the remaining flour with the cocoa, baking powder, soda and salt. Add to the creamed mixture, alternately with the water. Mix thoroughly, then stir in the sauerkraut. Grease and flour two 8 inch × 2 inch-deep layer pans. Divide the mixture evenly between them. Bake at 350° F/180° C/Gas 4 for 35–40 minutes or until the cakes are springy and test 'done' when a thin hot skewer is inserted. Cool for ten minutes in the pans, then turn out carefully on to a wire rack. A modern variation is to fill the cake with cinnamon buttercream (or cinnamon-flavoured applesauce if you prefer) when quite cold. Dust the top with cinnamon-flavoured sugar.

Twelfth Cake.

Baba.

Tennis Cake.

Gateau.

Madeira Cake.

Margipan.

Rout Cakes.

Wedding Cake.

Shortbread.

Petit Fours.

Sponge Cake.

Christening Cake.

Fancy Cake.

Cakes.

132

PUDDINGS

The Green Man of Brighton

Henry Cope was known as The Green Man of Brighton. Picture if you can a man who wore green from head to foot – so much so that his face reflected all this greenery rather as a buttercup held under the chin reflects yellow. Such a sight was Brighton's Henry Cope. His carriage and groom were green, and his home was. It's a wonder he didn't feel sea-sick in his totally green environs. Needless to say he ate only green-stuffs!

I think his death is rather sad – walking one day on the cliff-tops by the sea, he came to the edge and just kept walking . . . .

GREEN . . .

You may think it difficult to produce an entirely green fruit salad, but by stretching the imagination (a good exercise for any eccentric!) and using a few drops of green food colouring with the following ingredients, anything is possible.

2 grapefruit, peeled, halved and segmented
$\frac{1}{2}$ lb seedless green grapes, washed and halved
4 kiwi fruit
$\frac{1}{2}$ a melon, diced
Few gooseberries

Sugar to taste
Green angelica leaves to decorate

Mix all these fruits together. If there is insufficient juice for the fruit salad, make a small quantity of sugar syrup and colour it with a few drops of green food colouring.

GREENER . . .

A green vegetable salad is of course easier. But you could try white cabbage (of course using only the outer, greener leaves) in a mint and yoghurt dressing; or avocado pear, crisp green apple, green pepper and a few chives/spring onions in a vinaigrette dressing. Easiest of all, of course, is any combination of lettuces.

Claim to Fame

Jack Gainsborough was probably as useless as an inventor as his brother Thomas was good as an artist. One day when Jack was young he produced an Apple Dumpling Tree by covering each apple on a tree with dough, climbing up a ladder and cooking the apples individually in a saucepan of water warmed by a chafing dish. His imagination grew more bizarre as he got older, but this is his only claim to fame.

APPLE DUMPLINGS

Peel large apples, divide them, take out the cores, then close them again, first putting 1 clove in each. Roll out thin paste, cut it into as many pieces as you have apples, and fold each one neatly up; close the paste safely. Tie up each dumpling separately, very tight, and boil them an hour. When you take them up, dip each one into cold water, stand it in a bason two or three minutes, and it will turn more easily out of the cloth.

LE BON CUISINIER

PAR

Léon SOUCHAY, chef de cuisine

OUVRAGE COMPLET ILLUSTRÉ

Joli vol. in-8°

300 *figures intercalées dans le texte*, 800 *pages.*

Prix : broché, 10 francs, franco.
Cartonnage dos toile, 11 francs. — 11 francs 50 cent. *franco.*

LE GASTROPHILE

ou ART CULINAIRE

Par PAPUT-LEBEAU

Contenant 275 recettes, 60 menus des plus nouveaux, suivis
de leur application et du dressage de pièces.

1 vol. in-18 jésus de 356 pages. Prix : 3 fr. *franco.*

LE MÉMORIAL HISTORIQUE ET GÉOGRAPHIQUE

DE LA PATISSERIE

PAR

Pierre LACAM

PLUS DE 2,000 RECETTES

Prix : broché, *franco*, 8 fr. 75 ; relié, 10 fr. 75.

LE CUISINIER PRATICIEN, ou la Cuisine
simple et pratique (3e édition). *Franco*, 6 fr. 75 ; relié, 8 fr. 75

ART

DE

LA CONSERVATION

DES

SUBSTANCES ALIMENTAIRES

PAR PIERRE QUENTIN & BARBIER-DUVAL

Ouvrage orné de gravures intercalées dans le texte

Un vol. in-18 jésus, 180 pages. Prix : 2 fr.; 2 fr. 25 *franco*

Norman St John-Stevas

Norman St John-Stevas, MP for Chelmsford and former Cabinet Minister, hides an astute mind and a good intellect behind a veneer of comparative frivolity and is perhaps rather hurt when people take him at face value. He is a charming and thoughtful man with a range of interests far wider than that of the average politician – which is perhaps why he is more interesting and likable than many of his fellow-MPs. He is, almost inevitably, an excellent host and this is one of the puddings served at his dinner parties.

BANANA AND RUM ICE CREAM

4 ripe bananas, peeled and mashed
1 egg white
6 tbsps of rum
1 cup of single cream
1 cup of milk
pinch of salt

Blend the rum with the bananas and add the pinch of salt. Stiffly whisk the egg white and fold in. Stir in the cream and milk very slowly (best done in a blender at medium speed). Pour mixture into freezing tray. The refrigerator should be at coldest setting. When half-frozen remove and stir at once. Re-freeze until firm.

CHAPTER XX.

Boiled Puddings.

GENERAL DIRECTIONS.

Al Fresco

Here is a marvellous recipe with which Clotworthy Skeffington (see p. 95) might well have finished one of his banquets. By the way, he might have eaten this 'up on the roof', for the Earl often took a fancy to eating alfresco. He would have the dining table laid and then taken on to the roof with chairs for his guests and all the food, wine, crockery and cutlery for the meal. More often than not, however, he would then order the whole lot to be returned to the dining-room, where the meal would proceed as normally as possible after such an escapade.

TOURTE AUX POMMES

Puff paste, apples, to every lb of unpared apples allow 2 oz of moist sugar, $\frac{1}{2}$ teaspoonful of finely-minced lemon-peel, 1 tablespoonful of lemon-juice.

Make half a pound of puff-paste; place a border of it round the edge of a pie-dish and fill it with apples, pared, cored and cut into slices; sweeten with moist sugar, add the lemon-peel and juice, and 2 or 3 tablespoonfuls of water; cover with crust; cut it evenly round close to the edge of the pie-dish, and bake in a hot oven from half to three-quarters of an hour, or rather longer, should the pie be very large. When it is three-parts done, take it out of the oven, put the white of an egg on a plate, and, with the blade of a knife, whisk it to a froth; brush the pie over with this, then sprinkle upon it some sifted sugar and then a few drops of water. Put the pie back into the oven, and finish baking, and be particularly careful that it does not catch or burn, which it is very liable to do after the crust is iced. If made with a plain crust, the icing may be omitted. Allow 2 lb of apples for a tart for 6 persons.

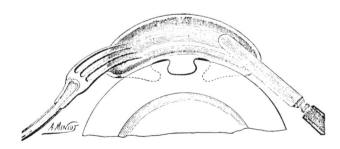

Christopher Biggins

Christopher Biggins must surely have more friends than anyone else in London. This cuddly actor, with the owl-like specs, is often to be found wining and dining at some of London's most fashionable restaurants including, I am pleased to say, my own. However Biggins is also an excellent cook and frequently entertains his friends to dinner at home where he often rounds off the meal with this delicious classic pud.

CREME BRULEE

2½ pints single cream
3 level tbsps vanilla essence

12 egg yolks
2 level tbsps caster sugar

Put the cream in the top half of a large double boiler or in a bowl over a pan of gently simmering water. Carefully stir the egg yolks beaten with the caster sugar, and vanilla essence, into the warm cream. Continue cooking gently until the cream has thickened enough to coat the back of the wooden spoon. Strain the cream through a fine sieve into a large soufflé dish and leave to cool in the fridge. It's best to make the cream the day before your party and on the day make a toffee mixture and pour over the cream. Pop back into fridge.

Serves 12

SIC ITUR AD ASTRA..

Balloon Tytler

James Tytler became the first British man to fly when he ascended in the Grand Edinburgh Fire Balloon on 5 August 1784. From that day on he was known as Balloon Tytler, a title much enjoyed by a man who threw himself into projects with considerable enthusiasm but insufficient forethought.

Balloon Tytler lived a full and very varied life – training first to become a doctor, and serving as surgeon on a whaling ship in the Arctic. He was a member of the Glassites, an apothecary and a writer – editor of the second edition of the *Encyclopaedia Britannica* for 16 shillings a week in 1776, aged thirty. He frequently fled from one Scottish town to another to escape debtors and/or outraged wives. But I don't think he did all this in his balloon! What better recipe to give here than the delicious Edinburgh Fog?

EDINBURGH FOG

Cream, sugar, vanilla, ratafia biscuits, almonds

Beat half a pint of cream to a stiff froth with a little pounded sugar and vanilla flavouring. Mix thoroughly with a good handful of ratafia biscuits and some blanched and chopped almonds. Serve in a glass bowl or dish.

Jonathan Goodman

Jonathan Goodman has compiled the definitive theatrical reference book, *Who He?*, also known as *Goodman's Dictionary of the Unknown Famous*. Some obscure characters will have you puzzling long after you've read their entries and you will be forever dipping into the book to know more about the unknown. Who *is* Israel Baline?

Goodman himself has been called The Master Eccentric by no less than the *Sunday Telegraph* – a title not bestowed on any other in this book. He has also been called the greatest living master of true crime literature, and describes himself as a crime historian.

I am honoured, of course, that such a one should offer me his favourite pudding recipe, and leave it to him to introduce.

'I like gooey puddings, and like Indian Pudding most of all of them. I have been told, and believe implicitly, that it was invented by a Pilgrim Mother in Massachusetts. A couple of the ingredients provide the only two reasons I can think of for giving custom to a so-called health-food shop.

As I've spoken of Massachusetts, let me mention the breakfast that was served to, and apparently eaten by, the Borden family of Fall River on the sweltering-hot morning of Thursday, 4 August 1892; mutton *and* mutton-broth, sugar cakes, bananas, cookies, bread, coffee. A menu that, so it seems to me, gave the daughter, Lizzie, an adequate motive for chopping up her father and step-mother before lunch-time.'

INDIAN PUDDING

To make sufficient for splitting into half a dozen decent-sized portions, bring 4 cups of milk almost to the boil, then stir in two-thirds of a cup of molasses, half a cup of yellow cornmeal, a quarter of a cup of sugar, 2 tablespoons of butter, a half-teaspoon of nutmeg and of cinnamon, a quarter-teaspoon of ginger and of mixed spice, and a teaspoon of salt; bring the mixture to the boil, then simmer, stirring often, till it is thick. Scoop it into a buttered baking dish, pour a cup of cold milk over it, and bake at a gentle temperature (no more than gas mark 2) for about 3 hours. Serve piping hot, with plenty of double cream.

An Average Housewife?

Eliza Acton was born the daughter of a Sussex brewer on 17 April 1799. During her early life she was best known as a poet, and poetry was perhaps her first love, but it is for her cookery books, especially *Modern Cookery in all its Branches*, that she is remembered today. Her impact as a cookery writer was considerable. She was part of a trend away from the dominance of male chefs in aristocratic households towards a broad appreciation of cookery, and all other aspects of household management, as a largely female concern. Accordingly, her recipes may not have had the grandeur of, say, Escoffier, but they were bound to be more useful to the average housewife, and Miss Acton still managed to mention *truffles à l'italienne* and curried macaroni among her more mundane recipes. It seems likely that many of Mrs Beeton's recipes were based on those of Miss Acton, in which case the latter's influence on modern cookery is more immediate than had been thought. Eliza Acton's attractive style of writing enhanced the step-by-step detail of her recipes – her instructions to a beginner on how to make bread ran to over 700 words. In this she was typical of female cookery writers of the period, in marked contrast to male chefs such as Carème who left much of the detail of their recipes to the imagination and experience of their readers.

Clearly this forthright and successful woman was not lacking in a sense of humour and I think these next two recipes speak for themselves.

THE POOR AUTHOR'S PUDDING

Flavour a quart of new milk by boiling in it for a few minutes half a stick of well-bruised cinnamon, or the thin rind of a small lemon; add a few grains of salt, and three ounces of sugar, and turn the whole into a deep basin: when it is quite cold, stir to it three well-beaten eggs, and strain the mixture into a pie-dish. Cover the top entirely with slices of bread free from crust, and half an inch thick, cut so as to join neatly, and buttered on both sides: bake the pudding in a moderate oven for about half an hour, or in a Dutch oven before the fire. New milk, 1 quart; cinnamon, or lemon-rind; sugar, 3 oz; little salt; eggs, 3; buttered bread: baked $\frac{1}{2}$ hour.

MODERN COOKERY,

IN ALL ITS BRANCHES:

REDUCED TO

A SYSTEM OF EASY PRACTICE,

FOR THE USE OF PRIVATE FAMILIES.

IN A SERIES OF PRACTICAL RECEIPTS, WHICH HAVE BEEN
STRICTLY TESTED, AND ARE GIVEN WITH THE
MOST MINUTE EXACTNESS.

BY ELIZA ACTON.

ILLUSTRATED WITH NUMEROUS WOODCUTS.

LONDON:
LONGMAN, BROWN, GREEN AND LONGMANS,
PATERNOSTER ROW.

1845.

THE PUBLISHER'S PUDDING

This pudding can scarcely be made *too* rich.

First blanch, and then beat to the smoothest possible paste, six ounces of fresh Jordan almonds, and a dozen bitter ones; pour very gradually to them, in the mortar, three-quarters of a pint of boiling cream; then turn them into a cloth, and wring it from them again with strong expression. Heat a full half-pint of it afresh, and pour it, as soon as it boils, upon four ounces of fine bread-crumbs, set a plate over, and leave them to become nearly cold; then mix thoroughly with them four ounces of maccaroons, crushed tolerably small; five of finely minced beef-suet, five of marrow, cleared very carefully from fibre, and from the splinters of bone which are sometimes found in it, and shred not very small, two ounces of flour, six of pounded sugar, four of dried cherries, four of the best muscatel raisins, weighed after they are stoned, half a pound of candied citron, or of citron and orange-rind mixed, a quarter salt-spoonful of salt, half a nutmeg, the yolks only of seven full-sized eggs, the grated rind of a large lemon, and last of all, a glass of the best Cognac brandy, which must be stirred brisky in by slow degrees. Pour the mixture into a *thickly* buttered mould or basin, which contains a full quart, fill it to the brim, lay a sheet of buttered writing-paper over, then a well-floured cloth, tie them securely, and boil the pudding for four hours and a quarter; let it stand for two minutes before it is turned out; dish it carefully, and serve it with the German pudding-sauce.

Jordan almonds, 6 oz; bitter almonds, 12; cream, $\frac{3}{4}$ pint bread-crumbs, 4 oz; cream wrung from almonds, $\frac{1}{2}$ pint; crushed maccaroons, 4 oz; flour, 2 oz; beef-suet, 5 oz; marrow, 5 oz; dried cherries, 4 oz; stoned muscatel raisins, 4 oz; pounded sugar, 6 oz; candied citron or citron and orange-rind mixed), $\frac{1}{2}$ lb; pinch of salt; $\frac{1}{2}$ nutmeg; grated rind, 1 lemon, yolks of eggs, 7; best cognac, 1 wineglassful: boiled in mould or basin, $4\frac{1}{4}$ hours.

Obs. This pudding, which, if well made, is very light as well as rich, will be sufficiently good for most tastes without the almonds: when they are omitted, the boiling cream must be poured at once on to the bread-crumbs.

GERMAN CUSTARD PUDDING-SAUCE

Boil very gently together half-pint of new milk or of milk and cream mixed, a very thin strip or two of fresh lemon-rind, a bit of cinnamon, half-inch of a vanilla bean, and an ounce and a half or two ounces of sugar, until the milk is strongly flavoured; then strain, and pour it, by slow degrees, to the well-beaten yolks of three eggs, smoothly mixed with a *knife-end-full* (about half a teaspoonful) of flour, a grain or two of salt, and a tablespoonful of cold milk; and stir these very quickly round as the milk is added. Put the sauce again into the stewpan, and whisk or stir it rapidly until it thickens, and looks creamy. It must not be placed *upon* the fire, but should be held over it, when this is done. The Germans *mill* their sauces to a froth; but they may be whisked with almost equally good effect, though a small mill for the purpose – formed like a chocolate mill – may be had at a very trifling cost.

Zandra Rhodes

Wierd and wonderful Zandra Rhodes may choose to look strange, but she is more successful than many more conventional-looking people. She is, along with a select few like Jean Muir, a lasting influence not just on British fashion but on fashion the world over. Although she chooses to dye her hair red and paint her face with strange patterns, underneath she is a highly-organized, hard-working and successful businesswoman with a string of awards to her name, including Designer of the Year.

The recipe she sent me for my collection typifies her whole approach. Initially it may look unlikely but on reflection it is a perfect example of its kind.

'This recipe came back to me as it is from my childhood. At that time coloured food was not the 'done thing', and I suggested to my Auntie Kath, who was cooking, that we should make a green rice pudding. When it came out of the oven the skin on the top looked like a cabbage leaf, and my mother refused to eat it. I'd more or less forgotten about this until I was reminded on "This Is Your Life" – so I've given it a modern update.'

CABBAGE LEAF RICE PUDDING

$\frac{1}{2}$ pint milk
$\frac{1}{2}$ pint double cream
1 egg
3 tablespoons pudding rice
2 tablespoons sugar
Knob of butter
Pinch of salt
Crushed cardamon seed
Green food colouring

Wash the rice and bring to the boil. Continue to boil for five minutes, then drain. Warm milk and add cream, bring gently to the boil, adding the cardamon seed and sugar. Cool slightly and beat in the egg and add the butter. Finally, add green colouring – cook as 'normal' rice pudding!

This pudding can also be served cold with a sprig of mint, and side serving of mint ice cream, or green morello cherries.

Benedictine Ice Pudding.

Cream Ice.

Lemon Ice.

Clear Jelly.

Gateau.

Compôte of Oranges.

Nougat.

Compôte of Pears.

Soufflé.

Meringue.

Pine Apple Ice.

Pear Ice.

Orange Ice.

Vanilla Ice.

Chocolate Ice.

Sweet Dishes.

Spike Milligan

Spike Milligan (Terence Alan Milligan), actor and author, has become a part of the British way of life. Indeed as a member of the famous Goon Show he is one of the favourite performers of the heir to the throne. Spike Milligan is perhaps best described by that over-worked modern word 'zany', but in his case it's probably an apt description. Who else could publish books with titles such as *Dip the Puppy, Monty, His Part in my Victory* and *Unspun Socks from a Chicken's Laundry*? Indeed, Spike Milligan seems to have crossed over the invisible barrier between comic and philosopher and although I confess I can't always understand the way he's going I am as intrigued by him as are many others in the country.

SPAGHETTI DOLCE

Spaghetti, cooked al dente, no salt (about 8 minutes)

5 oz carton double cream

Castor sugar to taste

2 tbsps brandy

Cook spaghetti. While it is cooking, mix together cream, brandy and castor sugar. When spaghetti is ready, pour over the cream.

Serves 4.

Syllabub is one of the most authentic and truly English recipes and dates back many hundreds of years. It was a great favourite with Charles II. This is one of Elizabeth Raffald's recipes, which seems to be concerned with cutting out the middle-man.

TO MAKE A SYLLABUB UNDER THE COW

Put a bottle of strong beer and a pint of cyder into a punch bowl, grate in a small nutmeg, and sweeten it to your taste; then milk as much milk from the cow as will make a strong froth, and the ale look clear, let it stand an hour, then strew over a few currants, well washed, picked, and plumped before the fire, then send it to the table.

This is a traditional Fowey Pie recipe as eaten by my Robin Hood ancestor Humphrey Kynaston at the Three Pigeons Inn.

FOWEY PIE

Line a pie dish with short crust pastry and then fill it up with separate layers of apple, thinly sliced onion and grated hard cheese to the top. Sprinkle with a little mace and spice and top with the same pastry – bake hot and eat as freshly made as possible – a real Tudor feast.

Here is a hunting pudding from Mrs Raffald for Squire Mytton. Just the thing to come home to after a hard day with the horses and hounds.

A HUNTING PUDDING

Beat eight eggs, and mix them with a pint of good cream, and a pound of flour, beat them well together, and put to them a pound of beef suet chopped very fine, a pound of currants well cleaned, half a pound of jar raisins stoned and chopped small, a quarter of a pound of powdered sugar, two ounces of candied citron, the same of candied orange cut small, grate a large nutmeg, and mix all well together, with half a gill of brandy, put in a cloth, and tie it up close, it will take four hours boiling.

Patrick Moore

This lovable television astronomer's eyes constantly appear to be following the constellations that others cannot see. His has been a real achievement – to make a subject like astronomy popular viewing for people who would normally run a mile from anything self-consciously intellectual. He is a keen member of his local amateur dramatic society and an accomplished xylophonist. The charm of Patrick Moore is that despite his immense knowledge and outstanding ability to communicate that knowledge to other people he is not in the least pompous – as his recipe demonstrates.

TRIFLE SURPRISE

Comb the larder, and rescue any passé cake. (Sponge cake does very well.) Put it into a jar, and mash it as well as possible. Next, look around all alcoholic bottles to see what is left. Whisky, sherry, vodka, gin – anything; even wine. Pour these on to the cake mixture. Shake well, and then store away. Leave (airtight) for at least 48 hours. Then serve with Devonshire cream and any fruit which is available. The result can be quite astounding!

150

"What a delicious looking flavour!"

10 Flavours

PEACH
PINEAPPLE
APRICOT
LIME
ORANGE

CHOCOLATE
LEMON
RASPBERRY F.P
COFFEE
ROSE

AS SCOTTIE SAYS FLAVOURING AND COLOURING MAKE ALL THE DIFFERENCE

Qualco
FLAVOUR AND COLOUR COMPOUND

If pastries look 'delicious', customers presume they taste delicious ... and they'll not be disappointed if QUALCO Flavour and Colour Compounds have been used, which flavour, colour, and glaze at the same time. QUALCO is available in ten delightful flavours and will help you to build, *and maintain,* in spite of present day difficulties with inferior ingredients, a reputation for the finest quality cakes and pastries.

PRICES

Cash with order . . 5/- per lb
10 lb. tins . . . 4/9 per lb
20 lb. tins . . . 4/6 per lb

Carriage paid

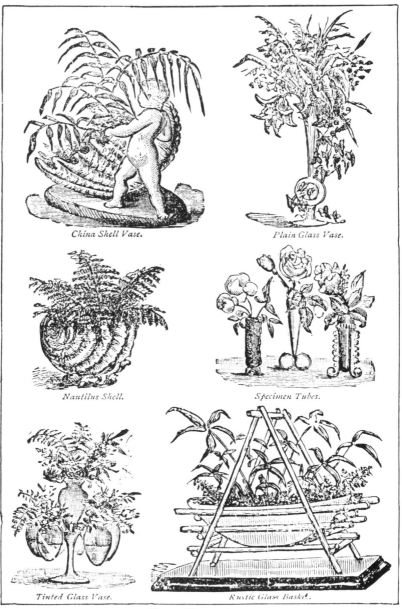

China Shell Vase.

Plain Glass Vase.

Nautilus Shell.

Specimen Tubes.

Tinted Glass Vase.

Rustic Glass Basket.

Table Decorations.

In the eighteenth century British cooks excelled themselves when making exotic puddings rich in alcohol and cream. Some of these recipes have far-fetched names – less attractive sometimes than the resulting article. Many of the best of them were found in Scotland, which for a long time was more closely connected with France than with England, a fact which is borne out by some of the best of Scottish cookery. Here are a few you may like to try.

HULLUAH

INGREDIENTS: $\frac{1}{2}$ pint of sugee or tous les mois, $\frac{1}{2}$ lb each of butter, sugar, pounded almonds, stoned and chopped raisins, a few ripe cardamoms, 1 stick of cinnamon, 1 pint of water.
MODE: Soak the grain in the water for 12, or if in winter, for 18 hours, strain through a coarse duster, removing only such impurities as remain unstrained. Add to this the sugar, put it in a lined saucepan over the fire, and as it comes to the boil, add the other ingredients one at a time, stirring all the while till it thickens. Pour into oiled shapes, and when cold turn out.

A HEDGEHOG

Almonds, sack or orange-flower water, eggs, cream, butter, currants.

Blanch and beat a pound of almonds very fine with a spoonful of sack or orange-flower water to keep them from oiling; make it into a stiff paste, then beat up six eggs and put two whites; sweeten it with fine sugar, then put in half a mutchkin of cream and a quarter of a pound of beat butter; set it on your stove and keep it stirring till it is so stiff that you can make it into the shape of a hedgehog, then stick it full of blanched almonds cut in straws; set them on like the bristles with two currants plumped for eyes, then place it in the middle of the dish and boil some cream; put in it the yolks of two eggs and sweeten it to your taste; put it on a slow fire and when it is scalding hot take it off; you must keep it stirring all the while; when it is cold put it about the hedgehog.

A HEN'S NEST

Calves-foot jelly, blancmange, lemon peel, egg-shells

Take calves-foot jelly that is very strong and put it in a white bowl or a Turk's-cap, fill it near half-full of the jelly, let it be cold; take five eggs, make a hole in the narrow end of them that the yolks and whites may come out; then fill them with blancmange; let them stand till they are cold, then take off the shells by pieces and take care not to break the blancmange; then lay them in the middle of the jelly so that they don't touch one another; then pour more jelly on them when it is almost cold. Cut some lemon peel as straws and, when the jelly is stiff, strew it over it; then pour a little more jelly over it. When all is cold and very stiff, dip the bowl in hot water. Have an ashet ready and put it on the top of the bowl and turn it out quick. Don't let the bowl be a moment in the water.

WHIM-WHAM

Cream, white wine, lemon, Naples biscuit, red currant jelly, candied citron and orange peel

Sweeten a quart of cream and mix with it a teacupful of white wine and the grated peel of a lemon; whisk to a froth, which drain upon the back of a sieve and put part into a deep glass dish; cut some Naples biscuit as thin as possible and put a layer lightly over the froth and one of red currant jelly, then a layer of the froth and one of biscuit and jelly; finish with the froth and pour the remainder of the cream into the dish and garnish with citron and candied orange peel cut into straws.

No. 1.

FANCY JELLIES.

Description of Belgrave Mould.

Figure No. 1, repre sents the mould in its entireness. No. 2, shows the interior of it (inverted). *A* is a thin metal plate which when turned down- wards forms the bot- tom of the mould, and which is perforated in six places to permit the fluted columns *B* to pass through it. There is also a larger aperture in the middle to admit the centre cylinder. The plate is fixed, and the whole

No. 2.

held in its place by the part which folds over the larger scallop *D* at either end. There is also a cover which fits to the mould, and which is pressed on it before it is dipped into water, to prevent its getting into the cylinders.

DRINKS

Pattisons' Whisky, like a British Ironclad, is at home in all "Waters."

ASK FOR { 'PATTISONS'' and Schweppe. 'PATTISONS'' and Apollinaris.
'PATTISONS'' and Soda. 'PATTISONS'' and St. Ronans.

A Calabash of Apatashe

There is a potent Ghanaian brew called pito made from millet which I came across during my time there. You didn't order a pint of pito, you ordered a calabash of it. There was also a filthy home-brewed gin called Apatashe, so strong you could fill your lighter with it and it still worked.

While I was teaching in Ghana, one Open Day the local chief came to the school. His name was Navro Pio and his village was called Navrongo. He had 100 wives and 350 children – half the

pupils in the school *and* two of the masters were his. I was showing this local chief around the lab, demonstrating magnesium flaring, litmus paper changing colour, etc., etc. Navro Pio could not understand any of the experiments, and I can't blame him. But we had a distillation demonstration at the back of the lab so I took him to it and poured him a sample of the distillate. Enlightenment at last! A broad grin spread over his face and he exclaimed, 'Ahh – Apatashe!'

It tastes not unlike apple brandy but I'd like to assure the Customs and Excise that we don't do it at Weston Park.

This story serves as a preamble to the subject of the Reverend Davis.

Reverend Davis

The Reverend Davis is an elderly temperance campaigner, who normally objects to any new licences being granted, particularly in the Westminster area, or any change of licence. He has opposed me at my restaurants at least twice, and in fact goes to great lengths to present his case and produce maps and show exactly how many licensed premises there are in the area and why they shouldn't be increased. The magistrates normally listen attentively and then grant the licence. In fact he's well liked and is occasionally successful. It was decided that his name should be immortalized for ever by naming a cocktail after him. It is in fact a most popular non-alcoholic cocktail as served now by most of the bars in the Covent Garden area, and I put it first in this section as a tribute to that resolute campaigner.

THE REVEREND DAVIS

Orange juice, pineapple juice, cream, dash of grenadine. Shake and pour into glass with ice.

This is also a non-alcoholic cocktail, a Victorian one. In those days a cocktail was known as a 'Popular American drink' and then, as now, most of them contained substantial quantities of alcohol. But this one would surely warm the Reverend Davis's heart.

CHING-CHING

1 good orange, a few drops of essence of cloves, ditto peppermint 3 or 4 lumps of sugar, a tumblerful of ice.

Slice the orange into a large glass, drop the essences and sugar on it, and add the ice, crushed or pounded.

Next, for something a bit stronger. There was this guy out in Los Angeles, I think, who used to go into his local bar and order a screwdriver with a shot of galliano. He used to consume enormous quantities of his drink and when he got off the bar stool, instead of going out of the door, he used to go straight into the wall – and that's how the Harvey Wallbanger got its name.

It is now one of the most popular cocktails everywhere.

HARVEY WALLBANGER

1 measure vodka, orange juice.
A float of galliano on the top of the glass.

SLOW COMFORTABLE SCREW UP AGAINST THE WALL

This is a cocktail that develops.
You start off with a screwdriver.
You then add Southern Comfort so that you have a Comfortable Screw.
You then add sloe gin so that you have a Slow Comfortable Screw.
You then add galliano so that you have a Slow Comfortable Screw up against the Wall.
More simply, it's a Harvey Wallbanger with Southern Comfort and sloe gin.

158

THE NEWPORT CODEBREAKER

Some years ago I tried to introduce a code of conduct for restaurants – which was referred to in the restaurant trade press as the Newport Code. The idea was that menus should not have hidden extras such as cover charge, VAT not included in the prices, rip-offs on vegetables, etc–that everything should be very clearly presented and if possible without extras. So the barman at Porters invented a cocktail to commemorate this, called the Newport Codebreaker. The joke of course is that it is the cocktail with *all* the hidden extras in it.

It is now a regular cocktail and our fifth-best seller.

THE NEWPORT CODEBREAKER

1 measure advocaat, 1 measure tequila, 1 measure light rum, 1 measure dark rum, 2 measures coconut cream, orange juice, cinnamon.

Blend all but cinnamon; pour and sprinkle with cinnamon.

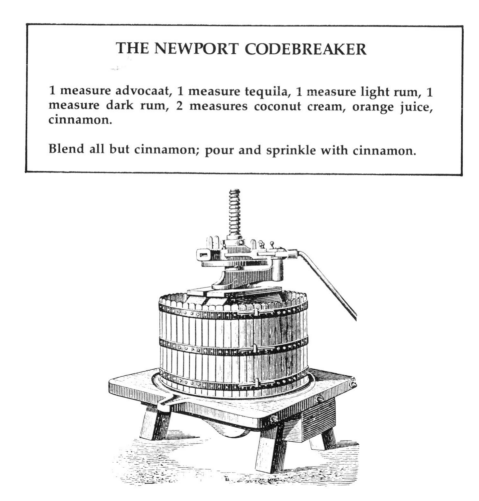

Here is a further selection of cocktails with eccentric titles devised and/or served by my barman at Porters.

ZOOM

1 measure desired spirit, 1 tsp cream, 1 tsp honey.

Melt honey in hot water and shake then strain.

STROUMF

2 measures gin, 2 measures apricot brandy, 1 measure amaretto, dash lemon juice, orange juice.

Shake and pour.

XYZ

2 measures gold rum, 1 measure triple sec, 1 measure lemon juice.

Shake and pour.

XANTHIA

1 measure gin, 1 measure yellow Chartreuse, 1 measure cherry brandy.

Build in glass and stir.

BRANDY GUMP

1 measure brandy, 1 measure lemon juice, 2 dashes grenadine.

Shake and pour.

Versoir belge.

BOSOM CARESSER

2 measures brandy, 1 measure orange curaçao, 1 egg yolk, 2 dashes grenadine.

Shake and pour.

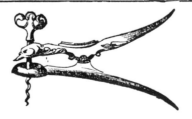

DUKE

2 measures Drambuie, 1 measure orange curaçao, 1 measure lemon juice, 1 egg, champagne.

Shake all but champagne, strain and top with champagne.

ITZA PARAMOUNT

2 measures gin, 1 measure Drambuie, 1 measure triple sec.

Build in glass and stir.

PRIZE IDIOT

1 measure vodka, 1 measure crème de bananes, 1 dash grenadine, 2 dashes lemon juice.

Build in glass and stir.

QUIET SUNDAY

2 measures vodka, 1 measure amaretto, orange juice, grenadine.

Shake all but grenadine, strain and add grenadine.

CORPSE REVIVER

2 measures brandy, 1 measure calvados, 1 measure sweet vermouth.

Build in glass and stir.

FUTURITY

1 measure sloe gin, 1 measure sweet vermouth, 2 dashes Angostura bitters.

Build in glass and stir.

Mrs Beeton strikes again. Here's what I think can only be described as a cocktail from the original version of her book.

FLOSTER

Ingredients: 1 gill of pale sherry, $\frac{1}{2}$ gill of noyeau, 1 oz of loaf sugar, 3 slices of lemon, 1 bottle of iced soda-water, 1 lump of ice. Mode: Mix all the above ingredients in a large glass, and drink through a straw.

Average Cost, 1s. 6d.

John Mytton

C. J. Apperley, Mytton's biographer 'Nimrod', wrote in 1835 in the Preface to his *Memoirs of the Life of the Late John Mytton*:
'as a private English gentleman, the world never saw before, neither is it, for some reason, desirable the world should ever again see . . . the anomaly in human nature which the character of the late John Mytton presents; at one time, an honour to his nature; at another, a satire on humanity.'
Part I also includes the, to me, fascinating paragraph:
. . . the first conspicuous ancestor of this family was, Reginold de Mutton, of Weston Lizard, Shropshire, now represented through the Wilbrahams and Newports by the present Earl of Bradford . . .

166

So I must claim some extraordinary ancestry here as well, and it was an Elizabeth Mytton who built Weston Park.

What a sport Squire Mytton was! He would not conform, and was expelled from both Westminster and Harrow. He never took advice, except perhaps once when his old teacher advised him to spend time at Cambridge, to which Mytton agreed, provided he did not have to do any work. Even so he did not go, preferring the Grand Tour. He had a brief career in the 7th Hussars, abandoning that to run the family estates at Halston and run for Parliament. His method of canvassing was to dress up to the nines and invite the electorate to pluck £10 notes from his gold coat buttons. His election cost him £10,000 (far more than he'd be allowed to spend today) and it is difficult to understand why he bothered, as his only appearance at Westminster was to be sworn in. It is not difficult, however, to understand how easily Mytton spent £500,000 of the family fortune in the seventeen years following his majority, for he would take no advice on money matters either and revelled in being open-handed and in the generosity which his wealth enabled him to show to others.

NEVER SUITABLY DRESSED

Squire Mytton was a madcap sportsman in every sense of the word. He hunted incessantly, and whether on horseback or in any sort of carriage he would jump at any obstacle rather than go round it. He jumped ditches, hedges, trees and rivers and swam lakes, sometimes for wagers, but more often for sheer devilment. Despite an extensive wardrobe, he was never suitably dressed for his escapades, often breaking bones because he

167

wore no protective clothing – favouring summer clothes or nudity for hunting!

Another major hazard in Mytton's lifestyle was his love of, and capacity for, drink. He drank port virtually from dawn until dusk. After his death a friend swore that Mytton had in fact been drunk for the previous twelve years. And he frequently shared his drinking, no less than his antics, with his animals, with whom he also shared an enormous affinity. He is reputed to have kept a thousand dogs, sixty cats, Nell, his pet bear (whom he rode about indoors until she bit his leg) and numerous horses. His favourite was one-eyed Baronet, whom Mytton saddled for some of his wildest escapades, including his leave-taking from the army, when they jumped the fully-arranged mess table.

Mytton had two wives: the first died after they had been married only two years and his second left him. It was soon after this that Mytton, imbibing increasing quantities of port, ran ever more seriously into debt. He was hounded by bailiffs and often imprisoned for debt. He died in March 1834 in the King's Bench Prison – of delirium tremens, I'm sorry to say.

Beware the demon drink and 'fast living'! Had Squire Mytton just done one or two things in moderation, he might have lived longer to enjoy his life – and his port with it.

TO MULL WINE

Grate half a nutmeg into a pint of wine, and sweeten it to your taste with loaf sugar, set it over the fire, and when it boils take it off to cool, beat the yolks of four eggs exceeding well, add to them a little cold wine, then mix them carefully with your hot wine, a little at a time, then pour it backwards and forwards several times till it looks fine and bright, then set it on the fire and heat it a little at a time for several times till it is quite hot and pretty thick, and pour it backwards and forwards several times; then send it in chocolate cups, and serve it up with dry toast cut in long narrow pieces.

1984 brought terrible news for the British, who consume more champagne than any other nation in the world. It seems as though the 1984 harvest would produce only 40 per cent of the usual quantity of champagne. Prices can only go up and you may well be grateful for the following nineteenth-century recipe.

MOCK CHAMPAGNE

To every quart of grapes, one quart of water; to every gallon of juice, allow three pounds of loaf sugar; half an ounce of isinglass to every ten gallons of wine, and a quart of brandy to every five gallons. Pick the grapes when full grown and just beginning to change colour, bruise them in a tub, pour in the water, and let them stand for three days, stirring once each day; then press the fruit through a cloth, let it stand for three or four hours, pour it carefully from any sediment, and add to it the sugar. Barrel it, and put the bung slightly in; at the end of three weeks, or when it has done working, put in the isinglass, previously dissolved in some of the liquor. Stir it for three days once a day, and at the last stirring add the brandy. In three or four days bung it down close, and in six months it should be bottled, and the corks tied down, or wired.

Edward de Bono

Edward de Bono is a controversial academic – controversial because he attracts a lot of publicity and that always seems to annoy other academics. He's the man who wants us to stop thinking in the same old ruts and to start lateral thinking instead. It's certainly done him a lot of good as he is now in great demand as a business adviser all over the world.

The following recipe was given to me by him and I think is a perfect example of his genre of thinking. Who else would have thought of combining coffee with curry?

EDWARD DE BONO'S CURRIED COFFEE

Black coffee, preferably of the Viennese variety.
Stir in an eighth of a teaspoon (for two cups) of Veeraswamy's curry paste.
Add a liqueur glassful of Grand Marnier.
Sprinkle with nutmeg.

The coffee's bitter taste pleases the tongue and foreparts of the mouth. The curry lingers as an after-taste at the back of the mouth and top of the throat. The Grand Marnier taste blends the two by creating a taste arch over the top of the mouth. The nutmeg blends the different tastes. The result should be sipped in small quantities. It tastes different from both coffee and curry.

Of course you think you've discovered something new in catering and you find out that Mrs Beeton was there before you. How did she do it? But she always did. Edward de Bono may be unnerved by the fact that over a hundred years ago Mrs Beeton came up with another curry drink meant to bring you warmth and good cheer on those winter mornings when you don't want to get out of bed.

FROSTY MORNING DRINK

(Comforting and Grateful)

Ingredients: 1 pint of good milk, 2 teaspoonfuls of curry-powder, sugar to taste. Mode: Boil the milk, add the curry and sugar and drink the mixture while hot. Time: about 7 or 8 minutes.

Average Cost, $2\frac{1}{2}$d.

Seasonable in winter.

Shrub is even older than Frosty Morning Drink but like it is meant to be warm and comforting. More an elaborate hot toddy than anything else, here are two versions you might like to try. And, as they say in all the best recipe books, for a smaller quantity, reduce the ingredients proportionately.

TO MAKE ALMOND SHRUB

Take three gallons of rum or brandy, three quarts of orange juice, the peels of three lemons, three pounds of loaf sugar, then take four ounces of bitter almonds, blanch and beat them fine, mix them in a pint of milk, then mix them all well together, let it stand for an hour to curdle, run it through a flannel bag several times till it is clear, then bottle it for use.

TO MAKE CURRANT SHRUB

Pick your currants clean from the stalks when they are full ripe, and put twenty-four pounds into a pitcher, with two pounds of single refined sugar, close the jug well up, and put it into a pan of boiling water till they are soft, then strain them through a jelly bag, and to every quart of juice put one quart of brandy, a pint of red wine, one quart of new milk, a pound of double refined sugar, and the whites of two eggs well beat, mix them all together, and cover them close up two days, then run it through a jelly bag and bottle it for use.

Proof that things don't change much over the years. The following letter from a Mr Desoutter was published in *The Times* of 2 February 1985:

Sir, Persons who are in ill health, or unused to rich food, should not be overwhelmed with an excess of nourishment.

The official view may be deduced from the *Manual of Military Cooking and Dietary* (1942). I quote:

'**Invalid Dietary.** When soldiers are required to attend their sick or wounded comrades, pending their admission to hospital the following simple recipes are useful:

Toast and Water. Boil 1 qt of water, and pour it on a good-sized piece of bread which has been well toasted before a clear fire until it becomes nearly crisp and of a dark brown colour; allow this to steep for $\frac{1}{2}$ hour, it is then ready.'. . .

Other equally delectable and restorative dishes follow, but Toast and Water was always my favourite – on paper.

Yours faithfully,

However, the army cooks had been pre-empted some 150 years earlier by a recipe called punnado.

TO MAKE PUNNADO

Take one quart of running water put it on the fire in a *skillet*, then cut a light roll of bread in slices about the bigness of a *groat* and as thin as wafers, lay it on a dish on a few coals, then put it into the water with two handfuls of currants, picked and washed, a little large mace, season it with sugar and rosewater when it is enough.

I cannot resist including this recipe for Stum by the redoubtable Elizabeth Raffald. If she ever made it then she is a truly great woman. If she ever drank it she is even greater.

TO MAKE STUM

Take a five gallon cask that has been well soaked in water, set it to drain, then take a pound of roll brimstone and melt it in a ladle, put as many rags to it as will suck up the melted brimstone, burn all those rags in the cask, cover the bung-hole but let it have a little air, so that it will keep burning; when it is burned out, put to it three gallons of the strongest cyder, and one ounce of common allum pounded, mix it with the cyder in the cask, and roll it about five or six times a day, for ten days, then take out the bung and hang the remainder of rags on a wire in the cask, as near the cyder as possible, and set them on fire as before, when it is burnt out bung the cask close, and roll it well about three or four times a day for two days, then let it stand seven or eight days, and this liquor will be so strong as to affect your eyes by looking at it. When you force a pipe of wine take a quart of this liquor, beat half an ounce of isinglass, and pull it in small pieces, whisk it together, and it will dissolve in four or five hours, break the jelly with your whisk, add a pound of alabaster to it and dissolve it in a little of the wine, then put it in the pipe and bung it close up, and in a day's time it will be fine and bright.

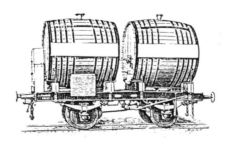

To conclude things on a personal note I include a recipe for mead as drunk by my highwayman ancestor Humphrey Kynaston.

MEAD

1 gallon of water
$\frac{1}{4}$ pint of loaf sugar
1 lemon (peel and juice)

1 pint clear honey
2 egg whites
1 oz yeast

Blend the water, honey and sugar, and stir in the frothy beaten egg whites. Bring to the boil and skim to keep clear. When lukewarm, stir in the creamed yeast. After two weeks add the lemon juice and grated peel, cover with a clean cloth and leave for three days. Bottle the clear liquid and store for a couple of weeks.